THE LIBRARY

COLBY JUNIOR COLLEGE

COLBY JUNIOR COLLEGE FOR WOMEN
PARATI · SERVIRE
MENS · ANIMUS · CORPUS
1837

S0-BRS-135

THE STATESMANSHIP
OF THE CIVIL WAR

THE MACMILLAN COMPANY
NEW YORK · CHICAGO
DALLAS · ATLANTA · SAN FRANCISCO

**THE MACMILLAN COMPANY
OF CANADA, LIMITED**
TORONTO

THE STATESMANSHIP

OF THE CIVIL WAR

by ALLAN NEVINS

DEWITT CLINTON PROFESSOR OF HISTORY
COLUMBIA UNIVERSITY

THE PAGE-BARBOUR LECTURES

UNIVERSITY OF VIRGINIA, 1951

NEW YORK   THE MACMILLAN COMPANY   1953

E
458
N45

Copyright, 1953, by The Macmillan Company.

All rights reserved—no part of this book may be re-
produced in any form without permission in writing
from the publisher, except by a reviewer who wishes
to quote brief passages in connection with a review
written for inclusion in magazine or newspaper.

FIRST PRINTING

Printed in the United States of America

34136

Preface

THE LECTURER TO A GENERAL AUDIENCE MAY BE PERMITTED, perhaps, to approach large and complex subjects with a boldness forbidden to the scholar writing for specialized groups. These three discourses, delivered on the Page-Barbour Foundation at the University of Virginia, are far removed from a formal treatise on the quality of the leadership exercised in the Civil War. They are exploratory in nature and tentative in their conclusions. Indeed, they are primarily an invitation to thought on the question of statesmanship in time of crisis, and a modest indication of some of the forces which elevate or depress statecraft. The author will deal much more fully with the subject, seen in its full historical setting, in two forthcoming volumes on the Civil War in his series called *Ordeal of the Union*.

Columbia University, June 1, 1953.

Contents

THE STATESMANSHIP
OF THE CIVIL WAR

The Conditions of Statesmanship

THERE IS A CERTAIN DARING PLEASURE IN PUTTING FOOT UPON a quicksand—if we can draw it back quicker than did Victor Hugo's Gilliatt in *Toilers of the Sea*. Such a quicksand lies in the word statesmanship. If we attempt a definition we shall do well to be ready to leap to the nearest *terra firma*.

As the year 1824 approached, Albert Gallatin looked about to discover some men who, as he put it, "could replace Mr. Jefferson, Mr. Madison, and himself"; that is, for another statesman. John Randolph was too eccentric. William H. Crawford had a powerful mind, inflexible integrity, and a correct judgment, yet he would not do. "Unfortunately," wrote Gallatin, "he was neither indulgent nor civil, and, consequently, was unpopular." John C. Calhoun was pronounced by Gallatin "a smart fellow, one of the first amongst second-rate men, but of lax political principles and an inordinate am-

bition, not over-delicate in the means of satisfying itself."
Henry Clay was a leader of splendid talents and most generous mind, but some doubts could be thrown upon his moral
character. As for John Quincy Adams, Gallatin thought him
"wanting to a deplorable degree in that most essential quality,
a sound and correct judgment." And of Andrew Jackson the
great Swiss-American declared that he was "an honest man,
and the idol of the worshippers of military glory, but from
incapacity, military habits, and habitual disregard of laws and
constitutional provisions, entirely unfit for the office of President."

From these judgments (and many similar to them could be
adduced) we may infer that no two men ever interpret the
term statesman alike; that seldom does a contemporary leader
seem a statesman to those who know him best—"Is Saul, also,
among the prophets?" scornfully demanded Saul's neighbors—
and that if Gallatin could go so far wrong on Calhoun, Adams,
and Jackson, we should not be cocksure in our own verdicts.

Yet, as John Locke bade us define our terms, some explora-
tion of the quicksand is indispensable. Throwing down a trial
plank, we can say that no *single* test of statesmanship is adequate. The ordinary rude test is success or failure. A statesman
is not merely a dead politician, in Tom Reed's famous epi-
gram (to reverse it, we might quote Ambrose Bierce's remark
that a politician, as compared with a statesman, "has the dis-
advantage of being alive"). He is a dead politician whose acts
and policies conspicuously succeeded. This *is* the popular test.
It was by the test of success that Lincoln fell short in the
spring of 1864, when Sumner, Greeley, and others complained
that he lacked the essential qualities of a leader, and wished
to see the Republican Party nominate someone else. At that

time not one of Lincoln's great policies had borne triumphant fruit. His selection of Grant as supreme commander still looked dubious, for Grant had been defeated in the Wilderness. His emancipation proclamation remained largely a nullity until the South was conquered. His effort to weld the discordant parties and factions of the North into a cohesive whole as yet appeared a failure. By the test of success, Lincoln was no statesman early in 1864, and a pre-eminent statesman in 1865. Woodrow Wilson was long discussed in terms of failure, although since the nation has turned back to his policies, his rank as a statesman stands unquestioned.

The fact is, of course, that no leader ever succeeds completely, and a mean success is achievable by any demagogue, while a grand failure is possible only to those with power to try the heights. We may dismiss the idea that a statesman is a successful politician with his bronze hand tucked into the breast of a bronze Prince Albert.

Because even the best statesman can map the future but vaguely, mere luck or fate will always play a certain part in permitting or withholding achievement. Solomon saw this long ago: "He that considereth the wind shall not sow, and he that looketh to the clouds shall not reap." So did Lord Halifax, quoted approvingly by Lord Morley. "He that leaveth nothing to chance," wrote Halifax, "will do few things ill, but he will do very few things." The fortunate leader thus gets praise beyond his due, and the unfortunate man often receives less than his meed. Van Buren and Hoover are lauded while their luck lasts, and mercilessly abused when the skies turn black. The truly vital questions are how high a leader aims, and how much he does to minimize the workings of malign fortune and to exploit favoring winds. The test is not whether a helmsman takes chances, as all men must, but whether, lucky or unlucky, his motives, skill, and prevision were of heroic quality.

And no condemnation by history is more emphatic than that which it gives to leaders who do not take their chances betimes. The odds rise fast against the timid. How they rose against America in the decade before the Civil War! Hoover and Sir John Simon would not take their chances in the Manchurian crisis of 1931, and the odds doubled. Baldwin and Laval winced before their risks in the Ethiopian crisis, and the odds doubled again. Chamberlain and Daladier retreated once more in the Munich crisis, and the odds had become appalling when the leaders of democracy finally had to take their chance in 1939.

As success is an inadequate test, so, too, is mere ability. Particularly among the English-speaking peoples, who prize the moral element in leadership more than most Continental or Asian folk, and who are stubbornly opposed to the Machiavellian prescription, does ability alone seem insufficient. "Mere ability" may seem a queer phrase, reminding us uncomfortably that the Tory Party hated George Canning for his "damned intellect." Nevertheless, it is a just phrase.

Said the younger Charles Francis Adams in his Lee Centennial Address: "The older I have grown . . . the greater in my esteem, as an element of strength in a people, has Character become, and the less in human affairs have I thought of mere capacity, or even genius." Bismarck is one of the immortals. He wrote his name in history by bold, effective strokes of the highest import. But he mocked at principles, shifted his allegiance when it was convenient, frankly asserted that a great aim justified the ugliest means, and made cynical use of intrigue and deception. What was he but the German counterpart of Richelieu?—and not only do both men seem wanting in moral greatness, but we may well believe that each, because of this deficiency, implanted in the polity of his country seeds of future calamity. Ability is important; but no Aaron Burr, Thurlow Weed, or James G. Blaine attains the name of statesman. Nor, of course, will character unbacked by pre-eminent ability suffice, else we should unhesitatingly call Sir Robert Peel and Grover Cleveland great men.

We require intellectual power; we require moral strength— weight of character; and we require something more—an instinct for the spirit and needs of a critical time. In eras of good feeling and quiet, and in placid, provincial societies, no statesmen appear; and every crisis demands its special leadership, of a type and quality for which the past seldom affords precedent. It is here that we meet the old insoluble problem of the relation between the great man and his environment; the question whether History is shaped by the Hero, or by massive socio-economic forces, or by both. Public opinion is constantly weighing leadership: "New Crisis Puts Solons on Hot Spot," runs the headline. Particularly in a highly articulate democracy is this ever-shifting adjustment between the leader and society of cardinal importance. The Politburo knows how to mold its own public opinion. But in our democracies leadership is dispersed among political chieftains, editors, teachers, writers, ministers, labor leaders, scientists, and businessmen. In a democracy various specialized qualities of leadership find a premium: eloquence counts for much, power of the pen for more, and parliamentary skill, expertness in party management, and governmental experience each have real if shifting values. But above all, the democratic leader needs, in Bryce's words, "the power to comprehend exactly the forces that affect the minds of the people and to discern what they desire and will support."

Gallatin, who is worth quoting twice, said in an address to the New York Historical Society in 1843 that George Washington's special qualities for his crisis were solid sense, weight of character, and an instinct for guiding the people. Washington was not particularly well educated, said Gallatin; he was far from eloquent; he lacked adroitness. But he had solid ability; he had character: "a profound and almost innate sense of justice, on all public occasions a perfect control of his strong passions . . . a most complete and extraordinary self-abnegation. Personal consequences and considerations were not even thought of, they were never thought of, they were obliterated." Above all, he had an instinct for the popular will: "The Americans had a right to be proud of Washington, because he was selected and maintained during his whole career by the people—never could he have thus been chosen and constantly supported had he not been the type and representative of the American people."

An event is a force momentarily made visible; a crisis is usually the product of a collision between new social, economic, and political forces and old institutions and ideas. A statesman then must be not only a leader of ability and character, but one who bears a constructive relation to the emergent forces of his era; forces much more easily defined by leisurely historians a generation later than by hurried practical men caught in the maelstrom which these forces create.

From time to time the fabric and outlook of every country needs a regeneration, and this usually comes about by the introduction of some great new social element into politics. The corruption of the British Government in Robert Walpole's day, and its rottenness, blindness, and inefficiency in Lord North's, were alarming to all keen-sighted men. Many Englishmen despaired of the nation. The situation in France under the feeble ministers and putrescent courts of Louis XV and Louis XVI was still more alarming.

In England, however, the corruption was gradually destroyed by the rise of an active new middle class built on mining, manufactures, and trade, which grew steadily in numbers, wealth, and power, and which brought with it a watchful newspaper press, an outspoken Dissenting clergy, and a body of authors, scholars, and orators who became potent molders of opinion. The new middle class, which was so busy making Britain the workshop, middleman, and banker of the world, had a stern Puritan morality and a deep-seated religious feeling—Quaker, Methodist, Anglican, or what not. The *Times*, the *Guardian*, the *Daily News*, and the other papers had a strong ethical sense edged by the radicalism of Wilkes and Cobbett; the literature created by Dickens, Kingsley, and Thackeray was a school of practical morals; and the new leadership typified by Peel, Bright, and Gladstone talked not only a good deal of cant but a great deal of courageous truth.

In France, the formidable front of corruption and class injustice sank beneath a different type of onslaught. The French Revolution gave birth to Napoleonic militarism and tyranny, with much else that was tragically unfortunate. But it also brought forward the massive power of the French people, imbued with emotions that went beyond hatred of a dead past and pride in martial glory; imbued also with an enthusiastic faith in man, an exalted if erratic belief in the des-

tiny of the human race. Before the French Revolution a statesman of the people was almost impossible; after it came a long
succession of them—Thiers, Guizot, Gambetta, and many
others down to Clemenceau.

So, too, in the United States only two generations after
Washington the political system needed a broadening regeneration. It came with the democratic forces of the Eastern factories and shops, and of the Western farm clearings; and it
found its statesmen in Jackson and Lincoln. Both men were essentially Jeffersonian in temper, though by no means always in
acts. Hamilton, John Adams, and such later figures as Daniel
Webster made the gravest error in misunderstanding and hence
underrating the emergent democracy of the West; just as
Jefferson had made one of his grandest contributions to statesmanlike growth when, impressed by the virtues of yeomen, he
strove to give agrarian democracy control of our destinies. The
Jeffersonian creed was not highly original. In its attempted
restriction of the powers of the national government it was
largely unrealistic, and so ill fitted to the demands of modern
times that in the end it gave way before Hamiltonian principles.

It had tremendous power, however, because it was a
formulation of popular aspirations, convictions, and interests.
And as Herbert Croly says, the Jacksonian and Lincolnian
schools were in some respects more Jeffersonian than Jefferson
himself, and sought to realize some of his ideas with more vigor
and consistency.

Now to divine the hopes, fears, moods, appetites, and opinions of a democracy in time of crisis, a leader needs an instinc-
tive understanding of the masses—a sort of sixth sense which
seldom comes without long experience; and to mold public

sentiment the greatest leaders need not only ability and character, but some kind of passion. Washington had a passion for independence and union; Jefferson a passion for equality and human freedom; Lincoln a passion for democracy as an example to the whole wide world. Even Hamilton had passion—a passion like that of Cromer in Egypt for governmental efficiency in the interests of the whole people. From passion alone is born an inspired view of the future. The impassioned statesman feels with Wordsworth at Rob Roy's grave:

> Of old things all are over-old,
> Of good things none are good enough;—
> We'll show that we can help to frame
> A world of other stuff.

Without passion, a leader may meet the problems of his day with sober practical wisdom, as Monroe, Polk, and Cleveland, strong men all, met theirs. But he can never meet them with inspiration; the inspiration that is the chief hallmark of a truly great statesman like Cavour or Lincoln, Wilson or Churchill.

2

We are thus brought to a question which I have never seen answered, though some kind of answer is necessary to our definition of the conditions of statesmanship in 1861. Why was it that the statesmanship of the Revolutionary era, our first tremendous crisis, was so much more impressive than the statesmanship of the Civil War era, our second? In the Revolution, three million Americans produced a galaxy of Olympian leaders—men who united practical political skill, a firm grasp of basic principles, and a broad vision of the future. Of the first Continental Congress, Lord Chatham declared that "for solidity of reasoning, force of sagacity, and wisdom of conclusion under such a complication of difficult circumstances, no nation or body of men can stand in preference to the General Congress at Philadelphia." Of the same assemblage, Lord Camden wistfully remarked: "I would have given half my fortune to have been a member of that which I believe to be the most virtuous body of men which ever had met or ever will meet together in this world."

It is quite marvelous that Revolutionary Virginia alone should have produced at least four men of truly statesmanlike stature: Washington, Jefferson, Madison, and George Mason —a few years more, and we could add John Marshall. Pennsylvania gave us Benjamin Franklin and James Wilson; New York, Alexander Hamilton and Gouverneur Morris; and New England, Roger Sherman and John Adams—to name no more. This is a roster which, in its combination of practical power and theoretical wisdom, is unmatched in the morning hour of any other nation.

How different were the fruits of the Civil War crisis! Thirty million Americans then encountered an ordeal as fierce, dangerous, and, if we include Reconstruction, as prolonged as the Revolutionary test; yet it yielded far less of statesmanship. One transcendent name indeed appears. To most Americans Lincoln seems as illustrious a personage as Washington, and if his figure has less majesty, its spell over plain folk throughout the world is even greater. Their statues stand side by side in the center of London. They are enshrined together in the hearts of lovers of freedom. But apart from

Lincoln, the Civil War produced no commanding governmental figures. Whatever the rank we give to Seward, Stanton,
and Chase, to Jefferson Davis, Alexander H. Stephens, and
Judah P. Benjamin, we cannot lift them to the plane of the
greater Revolutionary leaders. As constructive builders, as
vindicators of shining principles, as prophets whose inspiration broods over a succeeding era, they are far less impressive
than Washington, Franklin, John Adams, and Hamilton. Why
is this?

No doubt numerous reasons might be assigned. It gives us
pause to reflect that perhaps American democracy in the
period 1789–1860, in raising the level of average political par-
ticipation, depressed the level of exceptional leaders. As equality gained, so did mediocrity. One main reason, however, is
connected with this essential quality of passion or inspiration
in the greatest statesmen. The crisis which does most to evoke
that divine element is one which not merely calls forth all the
energies and talents a people can muster; which not merely
renders society plastic and malleable; which not merely ends
triumphantly, so that defensive action can pass into constructive action. It is a crisis which seems to throw open the gates
to a bright new future for a nation or for mankind; which
kindles faith that a refulgent era is dawning. The inspiring
crisis has always something of the poet's dream of an hour
in which 'twas bliss to be alive.

This was the hallowing character of the Revolutionary
crisis. Washington, Franklin, Jefferson, Madison, and Adams
were not contending merely for American independence; they
believed they were throwing open the gates upon a brighter
epoch for all mankind. They began, in Jefferson's words, to
"make a communication of grandeur and freedom" to other

peoples. "It is comfortable to see the standard of reason at length erected after so many ages during which the human mind has been held in vassalage by kings, priests, and nobles; and it is honorable for us to have produced the first legislature who had the courage to declare that the reason of man may be trusted with the formation of his own opinions." The leaders of the Revolution had faith that they were reshaping American society as an object lesson to all other peoples.

Possessed with an idea of the indefinite perfectibility of human nature, they thought anything possible, and were exexalted by the sense that they were participants in a bright new creation. Nor were they wrong. The Revolution, internal as well as external, did create a nation resting on a broad principle of equality, political, social, and economic; a nation where men were to have equal laws, equal political power, equal education, and equal opportunity, as fast as such equality could be made practicable. This was more than a continental achievement. It gave new meaning to human civilization. It made our Revolutionary builders not merely national statesmen, but world statesmen—a fact later registered in Auguste Comte's calendar of great men, and in Frederic Harrison's revision of his list.

Very different was our Civil War. To a great degree it represented a failure of American institutions, reflecting a deeper failure of American life. It was an effort not to open a roseate new chapter in human affairs, but to keep that chapter from being clapped shut. Except in the voice of one man of exceptional power and vision, the war lacked the inspiring note that marked the Revolution. Out of its agonies, losses, confusion, and moral debasement it seemed difficult to create anything ennobling. It was a war not of Construction, but in the words President Taylor's son used for his enthralling war record, of Destruction and Reconstruction—a grim and saddening war.

That the Civil War did have a tragically poetic quality there can be no doubt. It lent itself to memorable poetry written by Walt Whitman, Longfellow, Emerson, Whittier, and Sidney Lanier, as the Revolution had lent itself to prose— to the state papers of the Fathers and the orations of Henry, Everett, and Webster. It was a war of brother against brother, each sure of the justice of his cause: the very essence of tragedy. It demanded mass enlistments of youth, and condemned scores of thousands to lay down their lives with the devotion hymned in Lowell's Commemoration Ode, and the gallantry celebrated in John Esten Cooke's dirge for Pelham:

> The living are brave and noble,
> But the dead were the bravest of all.

Fought on our own unstoried soil, it invested countless scenes from Gettysburg to Pea Ridge with heroic associations. Lifting Ethiopia to freedom, it had in part the significance of a liberating crusade. It culminated in the martyrdom of the most beloved figure of the century. But if the struggle was full of essential poetry, it was not a war that seemed to open endless vistas of progress and to create a hopeful new world. In great degree, it was a record of the awful penalties of folly, incompetence, and pride.

This was the chief limiting factor in the statesmanship of the Civil War—the tragically negative and destructive nature of the crisis, to which Lincoln alone rose superior. But there were other limitations which we must scrutinize. As I have suggested, American democracy in 1860 did not stand at the happiest stage of its development. Both North and South, but particularly in the largest Northern cities and in the more impoverished Southern districts, power had been entrusted to the masses without a proper effort to educate them for its use. The country had too much illiteracy—a rising foreign-born illiteracy in the North, a sad, though fortunately de-decreasing, native white illiteracy in the South. Illiterates, and common-schooled but really uneducated voters, accounted for the sway of too many blatant demagogues like Fernando Wood in New York and A. G. Brown in Mississippi. The tone of public morals among those who cheered the Ben Butlers and the Louis T. Wigfalls illustrated a saying of Tocqueville at the time Napoleon III was meeting his first brilliant successes: "The world is a curious theatre, and *there are occasions when the worst pieces succeed best.*" That was true, for example, of some States and cities which temporarily fell under Know-Nothing control, and very true of South Carolina as the Rhett-Pickens school of fire-eaters seized the sceptre.

Then, too, one of the grave limitations upon statesmanship lay in the fact that the country had grown up to face huge and complex problems, but had not yet grown up to the training of experts or the creation of even a rudimentary planning mechanism. The government met its issues *ad hoc*, and often at the last minute with a hurried improvisation by amateurs. No planning was done by Congressional committees. No planning was done by the Cabinet. From Taylor to Buchanan inclusive, no planning worthy of the name was done by a President.

In England, the Ministry usually had to have a program of legislation, and hence had in some degree to mature a plan—although the way in which England blundered into the Crimean War, and the bungling amateurishness with which she fought it, were appalling. In America neither Pierce nor Buchanan ever had a legislative program. The most fateful measure of the decade preceding the war, the Kansas-Nebraska Act, was the work of one man, thrown together in a fortnight, amended in a few hurried consultations, and introduced with no attempt to measure its consequences. The lack of any machinery for thoroughly weighing and shaping policies, and the want of experts to help apply policies, crippled both Washington and Richmond throughout the war. Lincoln, Davis, and their respective Cabinets could attack exigencies with haste and blind energy, and sometimes by a *tour de force* conquer one. But the Presidential or Congressional commission was unknown; so was the unofficial adviser, the E. M. House, Bernard Baruch, or Harry Hopkins; and so was the man who made a true career of government as distinguished from a career of politics.

3

So far as statesmanship went, the ultimate problems of the North and of the South were vitally different in character. This fact, however, was largely ignored in the preoccupation of both governments with the *immediate* problem—that of winning the war. The tendency to concentrate upon military considerations can be illustrated by referring to the most imposing work produced by any Southern leader. Jefferson Davis's 1500-page treatise called *Rise and Fall of the Confederate Government* deserves respectful treatment, both as the product of truly heroic exertions by its author, and as the embodiment of beliefs and emotions poignantly shared by a multitude of Southerners. We need not concern ourselves here with its historical merits, or with its thorough, if otiose, treatment of constitutional questions on which honest men may hold the most divergent opinions. What is here important is the light it throws upon the temper with which Davis approached his task of leadership.

From this point of view, the most remarkable feature of the book is its almost complete silence respecting civil and administrative affairs. The distinguished author says almost nothing of the various departments—State, War, Navy, Treasury. He says almost nothing concerning political factions inside the Confederacy, and nothing at all about the public opinion behind them. He says nothing upon the problem of managing Congress. That his determined application of central controls aroused the most violent dissension, and that powerful groups led by such men as Zeb Vance and Joseph E. Brown displayed the most distressing insubordination, is an elementary fact of Confederate history. Yet Jefferson Davis seems intent on giving his readers the impression that absolute harmony reigned behind the Southern battle lines. The one area of civil government upon which he casts any real illumination is the financial history of the Confederacy.

This silence on civil policy was doubtless in part quite deliberate; the President of the Confederacy wished to defend himself and his section, not to pen a comprehensive history. But in still larger part it was a consequence of his wartime preoccupation with immediate military responsibilities at the expense of political problems and civil issues. Davis always regarded himself a military man. He had been educated at West Point; he had been colonel in the Mexican War, chairman of the Senate Military Affairs Committee, and Secretary of War.

In his own eyes, in 1861 he had a larger experience in military matters than any other American except perhaps Scott. The post he would have preferred was general of the Confederate armies. It was almost inevitable that when he became President, a civil official, he should take a much keener interest in military operations than in other subjects; and his memoirs reflect the absorption.

The main task of Jefferson Davis—as he well knew—was not to manage the detailed military operations of the Confederacy; it was to create a Southern nation. He well knew that in order to do this he would have to meet a flood of difficulties, and would in particular have to ride roughshod over the radical believers in State sovereignty. His main task tended always to fall into the background of his mind. Nevertheless, it *was* his main task, and his title to the name of statesman depended upon whether he performed it well.

In making a nation he had to act hurriedly, for his time was short, and to act in a revolutionary situation, which demanded revolutionary measures. For half a century most American Presidents had been administrators carrying out a few simple, well-understood, and manageable policies—and of recent years evading the biggest question of all. Now, in the storm of civil conflict, the Presidents in Washington and Richmond alike had to be bold improvisers—men who understood the cataclysmic nature of the era, and who, within the limits set by public opinion, could lead their peoples in the boldest action and the sternest sacrifice. Davis could make a nation only by showing some of the qualities of the great nation-makers: Washington, Cavour, Masaryk.

The principal responsibility of Lincoln was quite as difficult: it was the preservation of a nation. This meant not merely that he had to find means of bringing the eleven seceded States back into the Union, in itself a task demanding great powers of political, military, and moral leadership. Lincoln had also, while fighting a wasting, bloody war, to maintain the basic unity of a section divided among Democrats and Republicans, Radicals and Moderates, Unionists and Copperheads, Westerners and Easterners—a section swept by a thousand winds of opinion and prejudice, and subject in periods of defeat to terrible ebbs of morale. Preserving the nation meant maintaining at least a fighting minimum of unity and dedication in the North; the unity and dedication that ill-led nations easily lose, as Russia showed in 1917 and France in 1940. Lincoln never failed to realize that this was his paramount task, though he, too, gave more time than was proper to military details. He did not live to write a book of memoirs; but had he done so, it would certainly not have been chiefly concerned with the battle fronts, and would probably have said little about them. It would have dealt primarily with civil problems: with the departments, the Cabinet officers, his relation with Congress, and the civil decisions respecting finance, recruiting, and foreign affairs.

Through it all, we may believe, would have run a single binding cord, the cord of Lincoln's effort to rouse the finest impulses of the people; to teach them that in a successful republic the common citizen must, in Santayana's words, be something of a saint and something of a hero, and to justify Montesquieu's maxim that the principle of democracy is virtue. For that was the binding cord of Lincoln's effort.

Both Davis in trying to make a nation, and Lincoln in trying to preserve one, faced a fundamental difficulty, the lack of cohesiveness and organization in American society. The coun-

try over whose division Buchanan had presided in 1860–
1861, though fairly homogeneous in blood and language, was
singularly invertebrate and ill-knit. Not only was it divided
into four diverse sections, North, South, Border, and West,
but each section was loose and ungirt. It was to require an
industrial revolution, and a revolution in men's ideas as to the
function of the central government, to bind the nation tightly
together. When Tocqueville published his *Democracy in
America*, it was read by many as a treatise on two subjects
rather than one. It was of course the ablest study yet made
of the merits and defects of democracy, presenting the ex-
cellences with glowing cordiality, and at the same time point-
ing out dangers to be guarded against and weaknesses to be
corrected. But it was also an able study, again in specific terms,
of the question of centralization of authority and administration. If we look at John Stuart Mill's incisive comments on
Tocqueville's book, we shall see that he was as much inter-
ested in the study of Centralization as in that of Democracy.

Like Mill, like nearly all the political thinkers of the period,
Tocqueville was an antagonist of Centralization. As a consequence of his observations in America, Britain, and France,
he attached high importance to the performance of as many
community activities as possible by the people acting as individuals, without governmental direction or help. He believed
that only by restricting government within a narrow sphere,
and demanding that the collective business of society be done
in the main by private enterprise, could the latent capacities
of the people be evoked. Only thus could wills be braced,
talents developed, and social cooperation promoted. Only in
this way, too, could a strong barrier be erected against the
chief danger besetting democracy; the danger that, as in

ancient Rome, the principal executive officer should become a despot managing the destinies of millions who might be equals, but would be equally slaves.

In the period of Tocqueville, danger of the creation and perversion of despotic central authority existed in France, as Napoleon III demonstrated. Very little such danger existed in Britain. The British realm during the whole generation after 1840 was, as Mill expressed it, a country "where nine-tenths of the internal business which elsewhere devolves on the government, was transacted by agencies independent of it; where Centralization was, and is, the subject not only of rational disapprobation, but of unreasoning prejudice; where jealousy of governmental interference was a blind feeling resisting even the most beneficial exertion of legislative authority to correct the abuses of what pretends to be local government . . ." As for the United States, although Southerners had long worried over centralizing tendencies, and Northern Democrats inveighed against them, these tendencies had yet shown so little practical result that a mere handful of men transacted the executive business in Washington. The central authority was restricted by State Rights, by laissez-faire theories, by the inveterate suspicion of government born in the days of the colonial governors, and by the rapidity with which population had spread over wide areas.

As, in the political sphere, Americans of 1861 had the simplest possible mechanism of government, operated in amateur spirit by men who were amateurs in everything but politics, so, in the economic domain, central organization was almost completely wanting. Corporations were small; associations, societies, and trade unions were weak; no means of mobilizing capital for unified effort on a large scale existed; the sum total of all the men who had any real experience of conducting a large interstate business could have been contained in one ordinary room. The trunk-line railways belonged to the future, for the longest lines, the Erie and the New York Central, were each restricted to a single State. The corporation which owned physical property in several States was as nearly unknown as the corporation which held stock in several companies; indeed, not until the genius of Rockefeller, Vanderbilt, and a few others grappled with the problem after the Civil War, did corporations controlling a network of interstate interests become a reality. The churches were the only powerful nongovernmental organizations possessing a national character, and all of the churches but two, the Catholic and Episcopalian, were decentralized in administration.

Thus possessing only the rudest, simplest mechanisms, and served only by a personnel of amateurs, the Lincoln Administration and the Jefferson Davis Administration each had to create a Centralized Organization adequate to its colossal tasks. Improvisation—ever more hurried, spasmodic improvisation—had to be the keynote of both efforts. Even the stock of good amateurs was limited. Today we have a surplus of experienced, tested administrative and business experts, just as we have a broad margin of well-trained and experienced military and naval officers; hence it is difficult for us to conceive of the frantic search in 1861–1865 for men equal to their responsibilities. How should the two governments furnish food, uniforms, horses, mules, wagons, cannon, ammunition, for the hosts called to the colors? How deal with the sick, the wounded, the laggard? How coordinate the movements of armies scattered from the Atlantic to Kansas and Texas? And behind these administrative tasks lay the greater problem of welding a national sentiment. How could the two governments bind their respective peoples together materially and morally? Davis, in making a nation, and Lincoln, in preserving a nation, needed all the gifts we have enumerated as requisite to a statesman. They needed the capacity, the weight of character, and the self-abnegation that Gallatin attributed to Washington. They needed the passion, the inspiration, the dedication, of a Pitt, a Mazzini, a Wilson, a Masaryk.

Grappling with almost insoluble problems of organization, confronting a tenacious opponent, and compelled to sustain the morale of their peoples during four years of mounting loss and destruction, Davis, Lincoln, and their associates also needed another quality of statesmanship—patience, patience, patience. Each side had thought the war would be short. The very disorganization of the country made it long. Experts have said that if the national government had possessed a highly trained and fully equipped standing army of 30,000 men concentrated at Washington in 1861, it could have ended the war in a few months. But as the strength of one side grew, so did that of the other. The evenness of the two antagonists in fighting power made the conflict a test of endurance; and the leaders needed all the traits which Tolstoy's *War and Peace* depicts as belonging to Kutusov, who, like Wellington in the Peninsula, by patient, wary, unwearied action finally wore down Napoleon.

March of 1861 found the Lincoln Government, organized on the principle of recognizing in its upper personnel as many Republican factions as possible, at work in Washington: Seward, Chase, Cameron, Welles, Caleb B. Smith, Montgomery Blair—not one possessing any experience in his assigned department. It found the Davis Government, organized on the

principle of recognizing in its upper personnel as many Southern States as possible, assembled in Montgomery: Robert
Toombs, Christopher G. Memminger, Leroy P. Walker, Stephen R. Mallory, Judah P. Benjamin, and John H. Reagan—
again not one possessing any real experience in the department
under his charge. The cardinal test of Southern statesmanship,
by which we should measure the achievements and failures of
Davis and his associates, lies in the question: How much, over
and beyond the prosecution of the war, did their ideas, policies, and acts do to create a nation? The primary test of
Northern statesmanship, by which we should measure the
achievements and failures of Lincoln and his coadjutors, lies
in the question: How far, beyond the efficient prosecution
of the war, did their ideas, policies, and acts tend to preserve
the nation—to consecrate the people to the restoration of
national integrity?

Northern leaders did not comprehend the severity of their
coming ordeal until, as the army reeled back from Bull Run,
the press clamored that the country would yet be undone by
mere politicians. Southern leaders did not realize the full
magnitude of their ordeal until, as Farragut's fleet passed the
lower Mississippi forts, Mrs. Chesnut wrote in her diary what
thousands were saying: "New Orleans gone and with it the
Confederacy! . . . The Confederacy has been done to death
by the politicians." Then both sides girded themselves to meet
the deeper tests of statesmanship.

THE SOUTHERN DILEMMA

1

WHEN JEFFERSON DAVIS CAME TO DELIVER HIS INAUGURAL address in Richmond on February 22, 1862, and thus usher into existence the Permanent Government of the Confederacy, a note of pride crept into his brief recital of Southern accomplishment. The first year of Confederate history, he said, had been the most eventful in the annals of the continent:

A new government has been established, and its machinery put in operation over an area exceeding seven hundred thousand square miles. The great principles upon which we have been willing to hazard everything that is dear to man have made conquests for us which could never have been achieved by the sword. Our Confederacy has grown from six to thirteen States; and Maryland . . . will, I believe, when able to speak with unstifled voice, connect her destiny with the South. Our people have rallied with unexampled unanimity to the support of the great principles of constitutional government, with firm resolve to perpetuate by arms the rights which they could not peacefully secure. A million of men, it is estimated, are now standing in hostile array, and waging war along a frontier of thousands of miles. Battles have been fought, sieges have been conducted, and . . . the final result in our favor is not doubtful.

He added some words on Southern unity. "Never has a people evinced a more determined spirit than that now animating men, women, and children in every part of the country." This new national integrity, he predicted, would endure. "The recollections of this great contest, with all its common traditions of glory, of sacrifice, and of blood, will be the bond of harmony and enduring affection amongst the people, producing unity in policy, fraternity in sentiment, and just effort in war."

At that time, and for seven months afterward, President Davis's pride and optimism seemed fully justified. To be sure, by that date Missouri had been lost to the Confederacy; the blockade was being tightened all along the coast; Grant and Buell were about to start their advance in the Mississippi Valley, and McClellan to move his host against Richmond. The spring and summer of 1862, however, were in the main a season of Confederate victory. Grant was all but overwhelmed at Shiloh; McClellan's Peninsular campaign broke down in ignominious failure; Stonewall Jackson won in the Shenandoah the war's most spectacular victories against great odds. Lee was able in September of 1862 to invade Maryland, and Braxton Bragg to invade Kentucky. An able student of Confederate history, Robert Selph Henry, tells us that Southern fortunes reached their apex on September 17, when Lee's army in Maryland repulsed McClellan at Sharpsburg, while Braxton Bragg captured Munfordville in Kentucky, thus placing

the main Western force in position to effect a swift capture
of Louisville and close the Ohio. Their apex—for the tide
ebbed as Lee quickly retreated into Virginia, and Bragg
was checked by Buell at Perryville.

But, in this brief season of confidence, what were the facts
as to Southern unity and devotion? Before the war began a
high Southern officer, writing T. C. De Leon from Fayette-
ville, North Carolina, had declared that he was uncertain of
the temper of the Southern people under the branding iron of
grim hardship. "When the pockets of the rich and the bellies
of the poor are touched they will not be eel-like. They have
not been used to being skinned. The crisis will need a pilot at
the helm. A canoe and the *Great Eastern* require different
pilots."

While Jefferson Davis's inaugural address was still a theme
of general discussion, the Confederate Congress passed the first
Conscription Act. The law voided the control of the States
over all citizens between eighteen and thirty-five, placing them
under the exclusive jurisdiction of the President of the Confederacy. In thus striking at the heart of State Rights doctrine,
it deeply outraged powerful groups and individuals. Robert
Toombs pronounced the act unconstitutional. Linton Stephens
declared that it was hostile to the genius of American institutions; that it would "decitizenize" the troops; and that "if the
war last long enough under the degrading influences of conscription, they will come out of it utterly unfit for liberty."
Alexander H. Stephens termed it dangerous if not fatal. Zebu-
lon Vance of North Carolina burned with resentment, and
Governor Joseph E. Brown of Georgia presently asserted:
"No act of the Government of the United States prior to the

secession of Georgia struck a blow at constitutional liberty so fell as has been stricken [*sic*] by the conscript acts."

Such was one aspect of the difficulty of making the South into a nation, the primary task of Southern statesmanship; and other facets were equally troublesome. Even amid the first ardors and brightest victories, that unity in policy, fraternity in sentiment, and just effort in war of which President Davis spoke so trustfully were hard to evoke; in darker hours they became alarmingly remote.

The secession of the Lower South in 1860–1861 had been the product of varied forces, ideas, and emotions, among which sheer impulse counted for more than is generally supposed. Outside South Carolina, Mississippi, and little Florida it was sanctioned by very narrow majorities; indeed, it may be doubted whether a fair, sober, and complete referendum would have yielded any majority at all in Louisiana, Georgia, Alabama, and Texas. Nor is this strange. From one point of view, the headlong rush of the cotton States to form a new republic may certainly be treated as a confession of bankruptcy in statesmanship. It was rational only on one of two assumptions, both of which proved untenable: first, that the North would consent to the peaceable departure of the Southern sisters, or second, that although the North would resist secession, the ensuing conflict would be too brief for a heavy disturbance of the Southern economy and social structure.

Such men as Davis, Toombs, Iverson, Wigfall, and Slidell, who had spent long periods in Washington, should have known that these assumptions would prove invalid; Alexander H. Stephens and Judah P. Benjamin did know it. And if the assumption were discarded, leaders of the cotton kingdom should have seen that as a means of realizing their main objects, secession was worse than futile.

Secession actually enhanced the peril to the principal ideas and aims for which the Lower South had been contending. The leaders feared a sudden revolution in their social and labor systems; so they rushed into a revolutionary situation which made great and sudden changes unescapable. They feared that slavery would be exposed, after Lincoln's inauguration, to sharp attack; so they took a step which rendered sharp attack inevitable. They believed that the slaveholding regime could be perpetuated only if bulwarks were maintained which kept it in placid isolation from the evolution of Western society; and so they tore down existing bulwarks to expose their society, economy, and culture to stormy change. Even if secession had been peaceable, it would have brought Canada—that is, a foreign refuge for runaway slaves—down to the Southern border, and would have left the cotton kingdom more shelterless against world opprobrium and world pressures. This fact was pointed out by so good a friend of the Deep South as James Buchanan. He later wrote in *Mr. Buchanan's Administration on the Eve of the Rebellion*:

Besides, they were often warned and must have known that by their separation from the free States, these very rights over slave property, of which they were so jealous, would be in greater jeopardy than they had ever been under the Government of the Union. Theirs would then be the only Government in Christendom which had not abolished or was not in progress to abolish slavery. There would be a strong pressure from abroad against this institution. To resist this effectually would require the power and moral influence of the whole United States. They ought, also, to have foreseen that if their secession should end in civil war, whatever might be the event, slavery would receive a blow from which it could never recover.

"Whatever might be the event," wrote Buchanan, and he was right. For suppose the South had achieved victory. It could have done so only by the devoted aid given by millions of Negro slaves. They had refrained from revolt; so long as no Union force came near, they had remained soberly on plantation and farm; they had been indispensable in tilling the soil, mending roads, digging entrenchments, maintaining railways, and doing rough work in army camps and just behind the lines. And how would the South requite these faithful helpers? That question admitted of but one answer. The fact was that by 1860 the lot of the four million slaves *had* to be changed greatly for the better or radically for the worse. In a number of States harsh repressive laws were passed, and parties arose which even advocated enslavement of the free Negroes. But could the South, emerging triumphant from a war in which the Negroes had been an indispensable auxiliary, huddle them back into slave huts under the old terms?

By 1863, every thoughtful Southerner knew the answer was no. Robert Selph Henry calls the stand taken by the slaves "the highest tribute to the Southern Negro." The South would have to reward its faithful black allies and placate world sentiment by a sweeping program of reform—by protecting the slave's family life; stopping the interstate slave trade; giving him opportunity for education; and, in short, raising him toward freedom.

The fact was that the shot against Sumter doomed slavery no matter how the fortunes of the ensuing war went.

In still other areas secession really presaged a defeat of the aims of the Lower South. What of the effort to maintain an agrarian society with few manufactures and low tariffs? This, in an independent South, would have clashed with an inevitable movement to make the new nation self-sufficient. Davis spoke in his inaugural address of the progress of a single year, in commerce and industry, toward "making us a self-supporting and an independent nation." The Southern Commercial Conventions had laid the foundation for a Hamiltonian program, behind which the pressure of industrialists, bankers, railwaymen, and speculators would steadily have increased. Georgia would have striven to become another Pennsylvania, and Louisiana another New York. An independent South would soon have found planter and farmer lamenting new strides down the primrose path toward smoking factories, swelling cities, protective tariffs, and an industrial proletariat. Southern agriculture would have hurled the same plaints against Aiken cotton mills, Birmingham iron foundries, and Charleston brokers that it had aimed against Lawrence, Pittsburgh, and New York. Nor would it have been possible to avoid spasmodic increments in national authority and increases in taxation.

The refulgent dream which to many Southerners made all real and imaginary evils worth enduring was the prospect of creating a strong new nation. As painted by Hammond, Ruffin, and Yancey, a republic stretching from Virginia to Lower California, rich in indispensable staples of cotton, tobacco, and sugar, blessed with a harmonious society, and led by a natural aristocracy of talent, would forthwith take a proud place in the forum of powers. Rhett's eloquence and De Bow's statistical fancy described the recapture of the golden age. But how widely was this feeling of Southern nationalism shared as William Lowndes Yancey, welcoming Jefferson Davis to Montgomery, announced, "The hour and the man have met!"? Southern nationalism had certainly made no such progress by 1861 as the feeling of American nationalism had made in 1776. Even in the Lower South, as I have said, the best evidence is that fully half the population would, in a sober, fairly conducted referendum, have clung to the Union. As for the Upper South, it seceded tardily, reluctantly, and only for very special reasons. It had been divided on the expediency of secession even though it maintained the abstract right, and on the whole was against the step. But when Lincoln called for armed forces to coerce the Lower South—when he challenged the *right* of secession—the Upper South felt it had no alternative but to stalk through the open door. It left the Union because, holding that the States had never surrendered their individual sovereignty, it condemned the Federal coercion of any State.

2

No, in 1861 a Southern nation still had to be made; this was the chief task of the new government; and what were the qualifications of its leaders for the work? The South specially prided itself upon its political leadership, which most men believed to be its crowning glory. Had it not furnished the United States with its greatest Presidents, its ablest Chief Justices, and its most constructive Congressional leaders? Where could the North find names to match Washington, Jefferson, Jackson, Marshall, Taney, Clay, and Calhoun? It was widely supposed that now, in the crisis of 1861, a group of comparable statesmen would take the helm. The election of Davis and

Alexander H. Stephens seemed a good start. If the Cabinet unfortunately had to be made up on the principle of trying to give each populous state representation, each state nevertheless was hopeful its own son would play a great role; and Toombs as Secretary of State, Benjamin as Attorney-General, and Reagan as Postmaster-General had the advantage of well-earned reputations throughout the whole section.

Cabinet changes were early and frequent, Toombs being out of the State Department in about five months, and Pope Walker out of the War Department within seven. In all, fourteen men were needed in four years to fill six Cabinet posts. None the less, the Confederacy made singularly little use of some of its most talented sons. Howell Cobb, whose previous career had filled so important a page in national history, held no civil office at all. Toombs proved a misfit in the two capacities in which he was employed, and dropped into grumbling obscurity. Clement C. Clay, one of the South's brightest intellects, failed of reelection as Alabama Senator and spent a barren year as Confederate commissioner in Canada. Herschel V. Johnson, who did not expect the Confederacy to succeed and opposed every centralizing measure, occupied an uncomfortable seat in the Senate. Benjamin H. Hill, who took the other or national side on the principal war measures, held a seat yet more uncomfortable.

J. L. M. Curry had a term in the Confederate House, was defeated for reelection, and confessed that his wartime activities were utterly unimportant. No proper employment was made of the able Robert M. T. Hunter. The brilliant T. R. R. Cobb went into the army, to die at Fredericksburg. Senator Iverson sank without trace, and it would have been better for the South had Senator Yulee done the same, for his principal activity lay in preventing his Florida railroad from contributing much-needed equipment to the vital Confederate lines. Senators Mason and Slidell were condemned to humiliating failure as Confederate envoys abroad, and Slidell remained an exile in Paris after the war—"passing the remnant of a vicious and intriguing career," writes Gideon Welles, "in reading French fictions."

The men who, with Davis and Stephens, played important civil roles in the Confederacy, can be counted on the fingers of two hands. If we listed Judah P. Benjamin, James A. Seddon (the indefatigable Virginian who swayed the War Department in the darkest years of the conflict), Christopher Memminger, John H. Reagan, and Stephen R. Mallory, we should need to add few if any names to the catalogue.

Seven or eight men in all had the task of creating a nation behind the battle lines, and they had to do it with few of the ordinary aids. The development of a national spirit is primarily a moral and spiritual enterprise, which needs every intellectual talent. The South had no poets of the stature of Longfellow, Whittier, Lowell, Emerson, and Whitman, who all helped quicken the Northern pulse. It had no editors so able and devoted as Bryant, Samuel Bowles, Henry J. Raymond, and George William Curtis; indeed, several leading editors, like John Daniels of the Richmond *Examiner*, the Peter Porcupine of the South, and the two Rhetts of the Charleston *Mercury*, were highly mischievous.

It had no clergyman so eloquent as Henry Ward Beecher or T. Starr King. It yielded no pamphleteers so able as Charles J. Stillé, whose essay, "How a Free People Conduct a Long War," was worth half a dozen brigades to the North, or David A. Wells, whose "Our Burden and Our Strength" helped maintain, at home and abroad, firm faith in Northern victory. The South produced no song comparable with Julia Ward Howe's "Battle Hymn" and no piece of prose fiction to be mentioned in the same breath with Edward Everett Hale's "The Man Without a Country"; and it had no magazine so national as the *Atlantic*, which published Mrs. Howe's poem in February, 1862, and Hale's story in December, 1863. The whole burden of Confederate nation-making fell upon the handful of political leaders.

In administrative matters, right ably did most of them discharge their duties. Judah P. Benjamin had keen intelligence, permitting a quick grasp of intricate problems; he possessed versatility, imagination, and suppleness; protesting that he was an idler, he was actually a marvel of industry. Few men dealt with this ever-smiling, ever-polite Israelite, his silvery voice as charming as his cordial friendliness and quick wit, without liking him. Particularly did those susceptible to suave compliments find him ingratiating. He could meet the swifest change in a situation and cope with the wiliest of politicians.

His luck was bad, particularly in the Bermuda Hundred affair, which caused his temporary downfall, and his best biographer, Robert D. Meade, declares that for two reasons he was a failure in his most important post, the War Department. One reason lay in his unmilitary training and temperament, for the Confederate soldier Alexander Hunter spoke truly when he said that "Mr. Benjamin was a brilliant lawyer, but he knew as much about war as an Arab knows about the Sermon on the Mount." Certainly he never understood the military mind, created needless friction by sharp letters to proud leaders in the field, and harmed some vital military movements by petty meddling.

The other reason assigned for his failure is that he allowed himself to be too largely dominated by Jefferson Davis, failing to stand against the President even when he knew the latter to be wrong in his estimates of men and policies. Davis came to lean on him for daily companionship and counsel in much the way in which Lincoln leaned upon Seward, and the counsel should sometimes have been that of a frank no-man. These judgments, however, will seem to many overcritical. Benjamin was by no means wholly a failure, and considering his limited resources, in both the War and the State Departments he produced passable results. The two criticisms of him which really need emphasis are that he had no strong convictions about anything—about the rightness of the Confederate cause, about the conduct of the war, about large national policy; and that his influence counted for practically nothing upon the South at large, for it never passed beyond departmental walls.

On other Cabinet members the same judgment can be passed: they were efficient administrative heads who signally failed to exercise any broad Southern influence; they succeeded as workers but failed as inspirers. All students have agreed that in handling the mails Reagan did as well as could be expected with an impossible situation. Mallory, the ruler of an almost nonexistent navy, did better with it than anybody anticipated; his accomplishment, as J. T. Scharf says, excites surprise and wins admiration. In the War Department little can be said for Pope Walker, who began by haggling over prices when the Confederacy needed every gun and bullet it could obtain, who had little administrative capacity, who found the demands of contractors, politicians, and army officers intolerable to his fastidious tastes—"No *gentleman* can be fit for office," he groaned—and who in general shrank from the rough exigencies of the time.

By contrast, his successor Seddon, despite the ill health which made him the "walking corpse" of the *Rebel War Clerk's Diary*, shone resplendently. He had sagacity, insight, and energy. Whereas Walker, as Alexander H. Stephens said, had been "rash in counsel, irresolute in action," Seddon was cautious in counsel and resolute in action. No one can read his annual reports without being impressed by their grasp, shrewdness, and force. Then, too, as an administrator, Memminger evinced industry, devotion, and executive talent. This German martinet had long been chairman of the finance committee of the South Carolina House. Men could almost say of him what Disraeli said of Peel: "The right honorable gentleman's life has been one vast appropriation clause." He proved as good a Treasury head as any man could be who did not see beyond the end of his nose.

All the abler Cabinet officers were hard-working, single-minded, devoted servants to the cause; but not one—not even Benjamin or Seddon—burst from his office confines to rouse to higher zeal the mind and heart of the brave Southern people. Their government was a crisis government, their immediate task the meeting of one long, unending emergency; but they did not have even a Tom Paine in their ranks.

The Davis Administration taken as a whole was open, like all administrations, to grave criticisms on matters of policy. The grand blunder of adhering in 1861–1862 to the delusion that King Cotton could dictate peace, and that Southern interests therefore required an embargo on cotton for the economic coercion of Europe, has been the subject of unending controversy. Memminger, who foolishly thought the war would be short, after it became plain it would be very long, believed in the embargo; Judah P. Benjamin believed in it; President Davis believed in it and encouraged embargo measures at home while posing before Europe as a champion of unrestricted commercial intercourse. But it seems unfair to criticize the Administration on this head in view of the universality, or almost that, of the delusion. Congress, governors, legislatures, newspapers, and nearly every other articulate element shared the belief that if the South withheld cotton from export, Britain and France must in time forcibly smash the blockade.

A more direct criticism can be levelled against Memminger for not accepting the Congressional plan for buying the entire cotton crop and using it as a basis for both financial operations and diplomatic action. But Jefferson Davis was against this plan, and the plodding Memminger was frank to admit his own shortsightedness. Nine years after the war, replying to the strictures of Joseph E. Johnston, he explained that nearly everyone believed that "the blockade could not be continued for a year."

The fact was that, in its delusion as to the sway of King Cotton, the South was largely the victim of its own provincialism. It knew altogether too little of the contemporaneous world, the modern temper, and the new economic structure of Europe. Jefferson Davis was accurate in believing that there would be a cotton famine; he was accurate in believing that the Southern armies could hold the North at bay until this famine became acute; but he was quite inaccurate in measuring the probable response of the British and French working classes to the famine. He did not realize to what

effect Lancashire had read *Uncle Tom's Cabin*, or how powerful were the voices of Richard Cobden and John Bright.

Few Southerners had gone abroad, and still fewer had
gone as careful students of current tendencies. Most of the
South was old-fashioned and behind the times. It read Scott,
not Trollope; its literary criticism was based on the principles
of Dr. Johnson and Francis Jeffrey; its theology was unaffected by the newer scientific thought; in politics it still liked
constitutional disquisitions embellished by the rhetoric of
the Honorable Elijah Pogram school. Men truly cultivated
and really well-informed as to the contemporaneous world,
like Muscoe Garnett and William Henry Trescot, were rare.
One alert Southerner, William L. Yancey's brother B. C.
Yancey, had indeed returned in 1860 from an English sojourn
in which he had diligently inquired as to the probable attitude
of Britons high and low toward a slaveholding republic and
a deprivation of cotton. His conclusion was realistic—King
Cotton's sceptre was mere paper; but then B. C. Yancey
found no hearing in places of power.

Equal controversy has raged about the Administration's
failure to coordinate the Eastern and Western theaters of
military action, and properly support the latter. R. S. Henry
speaks caustically of its "usual policy of the dispersed defense
of scattered localities," which he thinks was particularly
disastrous when it compelled the Western command in 1862–
1863 to hold to the bitter end too many river posts, with the
result that garrisons as well as posts were lost. The greater
error, however, assuredly lay in the tendency of President
Davis and Secretaries Walker and Benjamin to concentrate
attention upon their Eastern fronts and ignore the Mississippi
Valley. A striking contrast can be drawn between the pains

the Confederate Government took in the early fortification and heavy garrisoning of Charleston, and its sad neglect of New Orleans, a port far richer and far more important, which was allowed to fall with no struggle worthy of the name.

The Western fronts were far distant: communication even by mail was slow and precarious; ground could be lost there for a time without touching other vital Confederate centers; and not until long after Shiloh was it clear that the Union had a commander of the highest ability in Grant. McClellan's Peninsular thrust demanded the most frenzied exertions by the Richmond authorities. It was all too natural, therefore, to neglect the West. The Virginia front was guarded by the genius of Lee and Jackson, and Charleston in 1863 defended by the high talent of Beauregard; but New Orleans had been left to the politician Mansfield Lovell; at Fort Donelson a divided command was headed by that still more egregious politician, John B. Floyd; and Vicksburg, the greatest fortress of the Confederacy, was entrusted to Pemberton.

Not until Seddon took charge of the War Department in November, 1862, and President Davis the next month visited the West, were systematic efforts made to coordinate Eastern and Western strategy. It is Seddon's chief title to fame that he made determined plans to strengthen the West and reshape its strategy—plans which under Joseph E. Johnston came to naught; and men will never cease to speculate whether the South might not have profited incalculably if the government in May, 1863, had followed Seddon's plan of sending a large part of Lee's army west to help drive Grant from Vicksburg, instead of using that army, as Lee desired, to invade Pennsylvania.

3

But these controversies over policy, however interesting, must not divert us from the central responsibility of the Davis Administration: that of welding the eleven States and nine million people of the Confederacy into a true nation. The brunt of this herculean labor unescapably fell upon one man, Jefferson Davis. Under our American system, the President always gives tone, character, and tendency to the government. An able, resourceful, farsighted President multiplies the faculties of even the ablest subordinate, as a weak President paralyzes their powers. An idealistic President does something to uplift his nation, and a vulgar President to vulgarize it.

Repeatedly we have had Cabinets of all the talents, as under Jefferson, Madison, John Quincy Adams, Polk, Pierce, Lincoln, and Cleveland; but always the question of their effectiveness in national leadership rested with the President. Polk's strong Cabinet did wonders, for Polk had a plan and an iron will; Pierce's still more brilliant Cabinet did little, for Pierce was as weak as he was charming. It was Davis's responsibility to make a nation because the whole South looked to him for that function. Since Calhoun's death he more than anyone else had been the voice of the South; he rose head and shoulders above his Cabinet; he alone could be the Washington of the newborn republic. Would his powers be equal to the test?

Let us do justice to certain rare qualities possessed by Jefferson Davis. The purity and elevation of his character have never been gainsaid. A proud, austere man, his mind luminous if not original, he had the approach of a statesman to public problems. In his prime (by 1861, alas, he was past it) he was a most commanding figure. Seward told William H. Russell that his brains, courage, and dexterity made him pre-eminent among Southern chieftains. His grace and dignity gave him a natural air of leadership, as Carl Schurz, a perceptive observer, records in his vignette of Davis when he was Pierce's War Minister. Writes Schurz:

He received me graciously. His slender, tall, and erect figure, his spare face, keen eyes, and fine forehead, not broad but high and well-shaped, presented the well-known strong American type. There was in his bearing a dignity which seemed entirely natural and unaffected—that kind of dignity which does not invite familiar approach, but will not render one uneasy by lofty assumption. His courtesy was without any condescending air . . . . His conversation ran in easy, and so far as I could judge, well-chosen and sometimes even elegant phrases and the timbre of his voice had something peculiarly agreeable. A few years later I heard him deliver a speech in the Senate, and again I was struck by the dignity of his bearing, the grace of his diction, and the rare charm of his voice—things which greatly distinguished him from many of his colleagues.

The depth of his convictions, as great as Calhoun's, exacts our respect even though we realize that in both men it was allied with a certain humorless fanaticism. No story of Davis is more revealing than that of his sudden heated protest, lying on his sickbed in pre-war days, at the badinage of that other Welshman, William H. Seward, a constant visitor whose facetious humor sometimes jarred upon the Mississipian. The New Yorker had confessed that he often spoke with jocose flippancy. "I *never* say anything that I don't mean!" Davis exclaimed. His dedication to Southern nationalism was complete. Infirm of health, tortured by neuralgia and insomnia, sensitive to hurts that a less finely organized man would have taken in his stride, he toiled with superhuman intensity; and, as a well-trained executive, he showed an efficiency in dispatching business that his great rival in Washington never approached. The South must always remember with special gratitude his magnificent cooperation with Lee.

It is unfortunate that we cannot say more for him, for this service was not enough. He failed to make a Southern nation—that, in view of military defeat, was inevitable; he failed even to make the contribution to that end which might have been expected.

In part the fault lay in his misconception of his true role. The before-mentioned preoccupation of his memoirs—apart from constitutional abstractions—with the military history of the Confederacy, is indicative of this. His greatest ambition in life was military fame, and his faith in his own military genius was so intense that he believed himself the equal of any Southern general. Men who tired of his repeated references to his famous inverted disposition of troops to meet the Mexican charge at Buena Vista were wont to say during the war: "If the Confederacy dies, it will die of a V." His wife records his heartfelt cry, so poignantly absurd, in an hour of desperate Southern peril: "If I could take one wing and Lee the other, I think we could between us wrest a victory from these people."

Jefferson Davis knew in his heart that his main task was a civil task, and not the management of the military affairs of the Confederacy, but he could never quite give himself up to it. A broad oversight of military matters was of course indispensable, but much more of this oversight might with general profit have been entrusted to Seddon and Lee. The frequent interference of Davis with tactical as well as strategic operations; his numerous expressions of personal pride and of irritability in dealing with commanders; his rasping quarrels with Beauregard, Joseph E. Johnston, and others; his favoritism toward the incompetent Commissary-General L. B. Northrop, and to Bragg and Hood—all these acts did the Confederacy a double harm. They often hampered military effort, and they took the President's mind from pressing civil problems. Every student of the surviving official documents of the Confederacy must be struck by Davis's attempts to control too much in military affairs, his approval or disapproval of innumerable orders and reports, and his dictatorial bent.

This readiness to forget his true central role went hand in hand with a tendency, born of stern personal pride, to act not for the current exigency alone, but with a gaze bent to some degree on posterity. When every ounce of his strength was needed for his daily tasks, he would take many hours to write explanatory or defensive letters addressed less to the recipient than to History. An example is the fourteen-page epistle to Joseph E. Johnston just after the fall of Vicksburg (July 15, 1863), which fills most of Chapter Forty-two in Mrs. Davis's second volume. Davis seems to have been right, Johnston wrong; but was this formidably quarrelsome letter worth while with so much to be done? To quarrel at all was a mistake; for as Plutarch says, "Anger turns the mind out of doors and bolts the door"—that is, it interferes with clear thinking.

The results of Davis's misapplication of energy and temper

soon became evident. For him, as for Lincoln, a critical election came midway in the war. Lincoln held his ground in 1862, keeping control of Congress; had he not done so, the North might well have lost the war. Davis, defeated in the Congressional elections of 1863, saw the legislative branch taken over by a hostile majority. Perhaps even the strongest and most tactful of Presidents could not have rallied a united South after Vicksburg and Gettysburg. Nevertheless, Davis combined a remarkable capacity for making foes with a remarkable incapacity for mobilizing friends.

The roster of his opponents became terrifying: Rhett, Yancey, Wigfall, Henry S. Foote, Beauregard, Joseph E. Johnston, Vance, Stephens, Joseph E. Brown, Yulee, Herschel Johnson, and many more. Some of them denounced Davis more savagely than the government in Washington. "Timid, peevish, and obstinate," wrote Stephens. The distilled venom of these enemies may be found sealed into the pages of Edward A. Pollard's *The Lost Cause*. It would be hard to name a worse piece of pseudo-history than Pollard's, a book so bad from every point of view that it should never have been published. It is not history but prejudiced and mean-spirited gossip. But it is surely significant that a volume so abusive of Jefferson Davis appeared just after the close of the war, and quickly found millions of readers. Still more significant are the scarifying passages upon him as viewed by the private soldiers in George Cary Eggleston's *A Rebel's Recollections*; "the grand master of incapacity," writes Eggleston. He had lost touch—sympathetic touch—with public opinion. By 1865, states R. W. Patrick in *Jefferson Davis and His Cabinet*, "perhaps half of his countrymen had little use for Davis and his Administration."

Varina Howell Davis, in her admirable work on her husband, admits this loss of control over public sentiment, attributing his growing unpopularity to the fact that ill-health forbade him to receive many people, entertain, or show himself much in public. "He was a nervous dyspeptic"; "he said he could do one duty or the other—give entertainments or administer the Government"; "in the evening he was too exhausted to receive informal visitors." She thinks that had he been physically equal to frequent meetings with Congress, the Virginia officials, and the people, his magnetism would have "mollified their resentments." Yet at the same time she admits that his magnetism was seldom visible. "He was abnormally sensitive to disapprobation . . . He felt how much he was misunderstood, and the sense of mortification and injustice gave him a repellent manner." Ill-health was no doubt part of the explanation—but the essential nature of the man was deeply involved.

His very real distinction of mind and manner, we feel, was built on too narrow a basis; his fine nature was too reserved, his elevated character too aristocratic. It could be said of him as of the second Pitt: "He never grew—he was cast." He was too intense and keen-edged, or, to use W. H. Russell's term, too drastic. In this respect he contrasted with the Illinoisan whose rich personality, wrote Lowell, offered no lonely mountain-peak of mind,

> Broad prairie rather, genial, level-lined,
> Fruitful and friendly for all human-kind,

and who won the increasing affection of the democratic masses. Mr. Douglas Freeman tells me that Robert E. Lee, viewing Abraham Lincoln across the battle lines, had the picture of a leader endowed with illimitable patience; that it was Lincoln's sagacious patience and persistence which gave Lee a touch of dread. Mr. Freeman also says that if he were asked to identify the primary trait which enabled Washington to carry the nation through the Revolution, he would name this identical quality of patience. The maker of the nation and its preserver were alike endowed with two magic gifts, utter self-abnegation and utter patience; gifts closely linked, for the man who thinks of self-interest cannot be patient.

The impracticable element in Davis's temper is revealed in his relations with Congress and Cabinet. He vetoed no fewer than thirty-nine acts of Congress, proof of the friction between its leaders and himself. Lincoln meanwhile, plagued by an equally factious Congress, went to the greatest lengths to avoid vetoes. He abandoned a contemplated veto of the Second Confiscation Act, knowing that the law would have meaning only as he and his Attorney-General enforced it. He gave only a pocket veto to the Wade-Davis bill on reconstruction, which he detested, and then took care to muster public sentiment behind himself in one of those closely argued appeals to reason which he knew so well how to write. Among the harshest critics of his policies was Charles Sumner; Lincoln made the difficult Massachusetts Senator an intimate friend, always welcome at the White House. When Sumner by a particularly mean-spirited maneuver thwarted one of Lincoln's dearest projects, the President sent him a note asking him to ride in his carriage to the second inauguration! We well know what Davis would have done in such circumstances.

As for Cabinet relations, Lincoln made but four changes in his official family, as against Davis's eight, and two of these were hardly chargeable to him; for the incompetent Cameron and lackadaisical Caleb B. Smith had gotten into the Cabinet as a result of pre-convention bargains made by David Davis and Leonard Swett behind Lincoln's back, and both in time were glad to get out. Lincoln prevented Congress from forcing Cabinet changes, even when in the crisis after Fredericksburg the most fearful assault was made on Seward. Davis, however, consented to the departure of Memminger and Seddon under fire, and even the sympathetic Professor Patrick, in treating the controversy with a Congressional group which led to Seddon's resignation, writes that the President's jealousy of his own dignity and want of tact were chiefly responsible. Reagan, Benjamin, and Seddon had much to say in praise of Davis when they retired. But they could never have uttered the immortal tribute which the long-surly Stanton paid to the President coffined in the East Room: "There lies the greatest master of men who ever lived."

But the principal deficiency of Davis as a nation-maker, the respect in which he most clearly falls behind Cavour, Masaryk, and Gandhi, lay in his want of passion. The great nation-builder must have some of the qualities of seer and poet, as these strong nationalists had; as even Bismarck, in his rough way, had. All these men could profoundly stir and inspire the hearts of their people. In his four years in Washington, Lincoln touched again and again the highest emotions of his countrymen. When did Davis, for all his devotion to a great cause, ever do it? He had a reputation for eloquence, but it was an eloquence cold, chiselled, and intellectual. Why was it that the winged words always came from the other side of the Potomac?

"Fellow citizens, *we* cannot escape history. We, of this

Congress and this Administration, will be remembered in spite of ourselves . . . The fiery trial through which we pass will light us down, in honor or dishonor, to the latest generation . . . We shall nobly save, or meanly lose, the last best hope of earth." What Congress would not be inspired by such an admonition? "General, I have heard, in such a way as to believe it, of your recently saying that both the army and the government needed a dictator. Of course, it was not for this, but in spite of it, that I have given you the command. Only those generals who win successes can set up as dictators. What I now ask of you is military success, and I will risk the dictatorship. The government will support you to the utmost of its ability . . . And now, beware of rashness. Beware of rashness, but, with energy and sleepless vigilance, go forward and give us victories." What general would not do his utmost after such an appeal? "Still, let us not be over-sanguine of a speedy final triumph. Let us be quite sober. Let us diligently apply the means, never doubting that a just God, in his own good time, will give us the rightful result." What citizen would not be more patient after that advice?

Such words, like those of Churchill in the last war, come only from a vision, generosity, and insight which were not in the devoted and heroic Davis. We cannot see how the South could have had grander generals than Lee and Stonewall Jackson, but we can easily see how it might have had a greater civil leadership.

4

Yet it would be unjust to lay the main responsibility for a want of passion and inspiration upon the deficiencies of

Davis and his colleagues. The final reason why this Administration exhibited so little of these qualities lies deeper than any personal limitation.

The South faced two great dilemmas. One, which has been treated so fully by historians that it is unnecessary to dwell upon it, was the practical political choice between State Rights and far-reaching, drastic measures for the survival of the Confederacy. Dr. Frank L. Owsley, examining what he calls the seamy side of Southern history in *State Rights in the Confederacy*, concludes that the South failed not because of overwhelming Northern strength, not because of the blockade, not because of any other external factor, but because of internal weakness. The seeds of death were implanted in the Confederacy at birth, he states, and these seeds were State Rights.

Jefferson Davis was an unyielding nationalist, loyal to the South rather than to Mississippi, ready to consolidate the Confederacy at the cost of State privileges, and bold in his strokes for independence no matter how angrily governors protested at some of them. He offended Governor Brown of Georgia, who was concerned with the defense of Georgia no matter what happened to Virginia or Tennessee; he outraged Governor Vance of North Carolina; he provoked Governor Milton of Florida to declare that he would rather see his State a desert drenched with the blood of its people than a vassal to Richmond. The first quarrel was over arms; had the States given them up freely to the new nation, the Confederacy might have equipped 600,000 instead of 400,000 soldiers by the end of 1861. A fiercer quarrel followed over the conscription of men; the States always kept large forces for local defense—perhaps an average of 100,000 much needed troops in 1862–1863. The bitter competition of the Confederacy and the States for vital supplies was meanwhile never ended; and when Lee's half-naked army fought its last battles with Grant, Governor Vance had 92,000 untouched uniforms in North Carolina depots.

The other and greater Southern dilemma was moral in character; and in it lies the principal reason why the Jefferson Davis Administration could never display the passion—the moral earnestness—which we find in Washington and Bolívar, Mazzini and Masaryk. The Confederacy emerged as a paladin of the ideas of freedom and self-determination. It also emerged as a great slaveholding nation; in Buchanan's words, the one important government in Christendom which had not abolished or was not in progress to abolish slavery. On the one side, it fought for a noble ideal of liberty; on the other, for the institution of servitude. It stood in an equivocal position on the world stage. Gladstone said: "There is no war except one, the war for liberty, that does not contain in it elements of corruption as well as of misery."

A thoughtful Southerner, Nathaniel W. Stephenson, wrote some years ago that the South had hopelessly compromised itself in not taking action, ten or fifteen years before 1861, to convert slavery into serfdom. Certainly it faced a crippling moral dilemma just after secession. For if it hoped to foster widespread foreign support, or to stimulate its own advanced and idealistic elements to desperate exertions, it must promise a grand amelioration of slavery, while if it made such a promise—as not a few voices even in 1861 demanded—it would hopelessly offend those who, like R. M. T. Hunter, exclaimed: "What did we secede for if not to save our slaves?"

Everyone is familiar with the protestation, "The Confederacy did not fight for slavery"; the argument, "Slavery was the occasion, not the cause, of the war"; and the question, "How could slavery have been the main issue when so heavy a majority of Southerners had no slaves and wanted none?" We all know that Robert E. Lee emancipated his slaves and pronounced slavery a misfortune; that Stonewall Jackson never owned but two slaves and gave both an opportunity to earn their freedom; that Joseph E. Johnston never had a slave and disliked the institution; that Matthew Fontaine Maury termed slavery a curse; and that A. P. Hill never had a slave and thought slavery a deplorable evil.

Unhappily, it is equally true that when the Confederacy was created many Southerners expected to bulwark and extend slavery. In the first Congress some designing men introduced a bill for reviving the slave trade; that is, providing that if a slave ship were "wrecked" on the Southern coast, the Negroes were to be sold at auction. Alexander H. Stephens's famous cornerstone speech was received with acclamation in much of the South, as with hot condemnation in much of the North and of Europe. "Our new government," he said, "is founded upon the opposite idea [to that of the Declaration of Independence]; its foundations are laid, its cornerstone rests, upon the great truth that the Negro is not equal to the white man, that slavery—subordination to the superior race—is his natural and normal condition . . . This stone which was rejected by the first builders, is become the chief stone of the corner in our new edifice."

The basic attitudes of the South toward slavery of course form much too complex a subject for brief analysis. It would perhaps be roughly fair to say, however, that the more enlightened Southerners were fighting for the right to deal with the joint problems of slavery and race adjustment in their own time and on their own terms. Most informed men realized that slavery was not an institution which would last forever; that soon it would have to be modified, and eventually, relinquished. They knew that the South could not maintain it very long after it ceased to serve a useful economic and social service, and that its utility was nearing an end. They wished, however, to choose the hour and method by which they should decree its gradual extinction. Knowing the complexity of the problem, they did not desire to be whirled into a catastrophic social revolution.

Why, we may ask, did the Confederate leaders not say this? If they announced that the new nation regarded slavery as a transitional system, and would soon study plans for abolishing the internal slave trade, legalizing slave marriages, and providing education for slave children, a host of Europeans might have moved to their side. "See," conservative Britons and Frenchmen might have said, "the Southern republic already goes beyond anything the North has dared to propose." Still more important, an announcement of this policy would have accentuated the Northern divisions. Even as it was, the Copperheads formed a powerful body, and the Laodiceans were numerous. Strengthened by such a pronouncement, the disloyal, the peace-loving, and the faint-hearted might, as Lee continued to win victories, have become irresistible.

But, in the light of thirty years of Southern defensiveness, the obstacles before so bold a step seemed insuperable. An announcement sufficiently strong to impress public opinion abroad and in the North would have shaken the Lower South to its foundations. There came a time when a more reckless, more desperate, or more convinced Confederate Government might really have acted. After Chickamauga in 1863 General Patrick Cleburne, appalled by the depletion of Southern ranks and the difficulty of obtaining recruits for the Western forces, prepared a careful paper advising the emancipation and enlistment of slaves. Letters in the Bragg Collection at the Western Reserve Historical Society show that this paper was signed by Generals Hardee, Polk, Cheatham, Hindman, and others.

Bragg himself referred to it as representing an "abolitionist" movement and as sponsored by the new "Abolition Party of the South." When early in 1864 it found its way by an unfriendly hand to Davis, he wrote that he appreciated the patriotic motive of the fourteen officers who had signed it, but that it was impolitic to make so controversial a document public, and he wished it suppressed. He knew that any decided step in that direction would split the South asunder. At this time even so mild an interference with slavery as the attempt of the Confederate Government to impress 20,000 slaves for labor purposes aroused the bitterest resentment. Governor Vance flatly rejected the national requisition, while South Carolina and Florida passed laws which practically nullified the Confederate statute.

The South was the prisoner of its dilemma. The one course Davis and his associates felt able to take was to remain silent—and silence implied the rejection of a constructive policy. Throughout the war the frozen taciturnity of Davis, Stephens, Benjamin and others on slavery gave Europe and the North no option but to believe that Confederate victory would mean the perpetuation of the institution; nay, would probably mean its extension over adjacent Caribbean areas. The government's blunder in sending Yancey as its envoy to England helped confirm that view, for England knew Yancey as an archdefender of slavery and an advocate of reviving the slave trade. John Bright scornfully repeated Stephens's cornerstone declaration in Exeter Hall. Goldwin Smith, the Duke of Argyll, Cairnes, John Stuart Mill and other sympathizers with the North made the most of similar proslavery utterances. As discussion of slavery had been tabu in the South before the war, so now it remained the skeleton locked in the closet.

Between the Scylla of world opinion and the Charybdis of Southern pride, sensitiveness, and economic interest, Confederate statesmanship stood immobile. Eventually it went to shipwreck on both. By the end of 1863 all hope of foreign intervention was gone, and by the beginning of September, 1864, all chance of Democratic victory in the North was ended. Yet the movement for the enlistment (and emancipation) of slaves had, without governmental encouragement, taken on strength. Late in 1864 General Lee was converted to it. Jefferson Davis himself finally came over. In a message of November 7, 1864, he proposed enlisting 40,000 Negroes for service, with a grant of freedom to all willing fighters. He also expressed doubt whether "the private right of property [in human beings] can consistently and beneficially be continued."

But desperate as the Confederate position had then become, the stand of Davis and the still bolder activities of Benjamin provoked a wild storm. When Benjamin at the famous meeting held at the African Church in Richmond on February 9, 1865, proposed a general enlistment of Negro soldiers, with the promise, "You are free," his doctrine was denounced as revolutionary, and Wigfall introduced in Congress a resolution that the country had lost confidence in him.

Years after the war ended Judah P. Benjamin walked home

from a Mayfair dinner party with William H. Russell. The journalist reminded the Southern exile that, when Attorney-General in Montgomery, he had predicted that within a year Britain would break the blockade. "When your factories are closed," Benjamin had then said, in effect, "when the Mississippi is floating cotton by thousands of bales, and all our wharves are full, it is inevitable that the Yankees will come to grief in the effort to coerce us." Russell, as the two strolled down Park Lane, spoke of the failure of the prophecy. "Ah, yes," responded Benjamin. "I was mistaken. I did not believe that your government would allow such misery to be visited on your workers, such loss to be inflicted on your manufacturers. I did not believe the people would have borne it."

The Lancashire operatives had borne it because of the weight of moral imponderables. They would not lend their support to a great slaveholding nation. They had pondered *Uncle Tom's Cabin*. They knew something of the history of the British antislavery movement. Their spokesmen in Parliament were Cobden, Bright, and Forster. And although their wives were ragged and their children hungry, they were on the side of human freedom. So it was with certain wavering segments of Northern opinion. Not least among the decisive battles of the war was this struggle for the control of British and Northern opinion, and not the smallest of the Northern victories was that won in the streets of Lancashire and at the Northern polling places.

The Southern republic indeed had the seeds of death implanted in it at birth. But there were two kinds of seeds—State Rights and slavery; and of the two slavery was the more important, for it deprived Southern statesmanship of all chance of expressing that passion, that soul-stirring inspiration which alone could make the new nation invincible and raise up friends for it beyond its borders.

If we look for inspiration, we find it, not in the council-chambers of the Confederacy, but on the battlefields; not in Davis, admirable as were some of his qualities, but in Lee and Jackson. In the end the two greatest acts of statesmanship were performed by Robert E. Lee. These acts of statesmanship were indeed among the most notable in all American history. When, after the fall of Richmond, it was proposed to Lee that he withdraw southward, take command of troops still available there, and conduct a protracted guerrilla resistance to the North, he had the statesmanlike vision and courage to refuse. He knew that such an effort to fight to the last ravine and last range of mountains would mean incalculable misery to the South as well as heavy loss to the North; that it would to no good end prolong the sorrows and intensify the bitterness of the conflict. Later still, it was Lee who did most to set a manly example of loyalty to the restored Union, and constructive labor for the rehabilitation of war-strained society. As the figure of Lincoln the statesman disappeared from the national stage, the figure of Lee the statesman momentarily appeared upon it.

Lincoln As More Than
A Statesman

IT HAS LONG BEEN THE FASHION FOR POPULAR WRITERS AND speakers to view Lincoln romantically, not realistically. Yet for regarding him realistically, without attempt to magnify or depreciate, we have this warrant, that he was himself a stern realist. He was a realist about his associates, Chase, Seward, Stanton, McClellan. He was a realist about himself and his limitations. "Money!" he exclaimed when somebody wanted to discuss war finances. "I don't know anything about money. I never had enough of my own to fret me, and I have no opinion about it in any way." He was a realist about the sweeping forces of the time, saying bluntly that he had not controlled events, but events had controlled him. He was a realist about the springs of public support, remarking sagely in one crisis: "I do not need sympathy nearly so much as I need success." He was a realist in always placing great objects above small ones. When the politicians protested against putting a new draft into effect in the midst of the presidential campaign of 1864, because it might cost him the election, he demanded: "What is the presidency worth to me if I have no country?"

Lincoln would have been quick to say that the effort to paint any man as ideal is absurd, and the first to dissent from many of the adulatory judgments of Nicolay and Hay.

The tendency to soften the lineaments of this strange, quaint, rugged, and powerful man has been natural, for his heart was as great as his brain; but it does injustice to his most important public aspect, his tough, forcible, hard-hitting side. Too much has been said of his kindness, mildness, and magnanimity. These traits were real, but so also were his calculating shrewdness, his firmness, his occasional harshness, and his infrequent but unforgettable bursts of anger. He said "no" with a good-natured air, but he said it often and positively. In dealing with cunning politicians he had a cunning of his own that Stanton called genius. He pardoned sleeping sentries and deserters not merely because he was kindly, but because he had a keen instinct for policy; he was no worshiper of generals, he disliked military despotism, he saw that the North had to depend on masses of volunteers, and he knew that if the regular army officers imposed the death penalty without check, volunteering would stop.

Not often, but more than once, he exhibited an ebullition of anger like Washington's at Monmouth. Donn Piatt, temporary commander in Baltimore, once gave General William Birney what Lincoln thought quite premature and damaging orders to recruit men for a Negro brigade. Piatt tells of the penalty he paid:

Then came a curt summons, ordering me to appear at the War
Department. I obeyed . . . Being informed that the Secretary
was at the Executive Mansion, I repaired there, sent in my card,
and was at once shown into the presence, not of Mr. Stanton but
of the President. I do not care to recall the words of Mr. Lincoln.
I wrote them out that night, for I was threatened with a shameful
dismissal from the service, and I intended appealing to the public.
They were exceedingly severe, for the President was in a rage.
I was not allowed to say a word in my own defence, and was
only permitted to say that I would countermand the order as
well as I could. I was saved cashiering through the influence of
Stanton and Chase . . .

Another misapprehension is all too common. Lincoln was
not a giant surrounded by dwarfs, and moving as a free agent,
with the other personages of the crowded drama subordinate
to his intellect and vision. Such a conception is subject to
correction on two counts.

To begin with, if Lincoln was unquestionably the greatest
of the Northern leaders in the Civil War, he was nevertheless
but the strongest of a group of great-statured men. The hard-
est work of dealing with the upheaval fell, under Lincoln,
to three lawyers drawn from the area between the Mohawk
and Maumee Rivers: Seward, Stanton, and Chase. Each, like
Lincoln, was (as we have noted) totally inexperienced in his
new field; each carried forward his work with blunders
aplenty, but with pluck, energy, and growing skill; each re-
fused to let it be obstructed or defeated; and each so exhausted himself that he emerged from the war with shattered
health, and soon died—Stanton in four years, Seward in seven,
and Chase in eight. Let us not underrate this powerful trio.
And, in the second place, Lincoln had to act within a tre-

mendous stream of forces, the chief of which were a Congress always headstrong and independent, and a public opinion of decidedly greater variety, turbulence, and force than that of the South—which is saying much. This Congress and public opinion had to be consulted at every turn.

In its more routine aspects, the special quality of Lincoln's statesmanship was its extraordinary realism or practicality. In his month-to-month work, what set him apart from Seward, Stanton, and Chase and above preceding or succeeding Presidents was his grasp of what was practicable at any given moment. He would never have reached national leadership but for this unerring instinct. Seward in the 1850's had rashly gone too far; he had uttered sentiments in his "higher law" speech and again in his "irrepressible conflict" speech which struck most citizens as excessively radical—and he failed of the prize. He forgot the truth expressed in Greville's maxim, "Only the Tories can carry Liberal Measures"—that is, only the man who is trusted can carry even the soundest measures if they originate with distrusted men. Edward Bates, in contrast, had not gone far enough in the 1850's; he had seemed lukewarm on the slavery question, and he too failed of the prize.

Lincoln had gone just far enough. He had been resolute on the two great principles of the wrongfulness of slavery, and the necessity of excluding it from the Territories; but he had stopped at that point. He had not risked offending cautious men by declaring what further steps he would take to put slavery, after its containment, in the way of ultimate extinction. That he left to time and the fit occasion. Throughout the Civil War he had a far surer sense than other men of the degrees by which revolutionary measures could be effected, and of the times for putting them into effect.

As his secretaries John Hay and John G. Nicolay put it, he was a great opportunist, in the good sense of the word, before the term opportunism was invented; in modern parlance, he was blessed with an uncanny sense of timing. He was, as Walter Bagehot said of Sir Robert Peel, the uncommon man of common opinions.

In his day-to-day work this realistic sense for the occasion, as the French call it, combined with his practical acumen in the leadership of men, much more than offset his manifest weaknesses as an executive. He was by no means distinguished as an administrator. Entering the White House without the slightest administrative training, his haphazard, unsystematic, unbusinesslike ways were the despair of secretaries and bureaucrats. His biographer John T. Morse correctly declares that "he had no capacity for business." His laxities were the theme of bitter complaint by the admiring Gideon Welles.

Salmon P. Chase declared midway in the war that there was no Administration in the proper sense of the word—that is, no coordination of the executive departments; and he wrote a friend in 1863 that when he wanted to know what was going on outside the Treasury, he had to send a boy out for a copy of the New York *Herald*. Lincoln gave close attention to the work of two departments, State and War, but with the others he seldom meddled, and his Administration was rather a loose coalition than a unitary body. He had no such capacity as Woodrow Wilson showed fifty-five years later in mobilizing the economic energies of the land. Their dispersed, unorganized character would have made the task extremely difficult, but we have no record of his interest in enlisting business-men and industrialists, and we may well wonder why the list of those employed—Thomas A. Scott, Peter H. Watson, the youthful Andrew Carnegie, Herman Haupt, and a few others —was not far longer.

Repeatedly, as was inevitable, he committed grave errors of judgment. Thomas M. Clarke, Episcopal Bishop of Rhode Island, called on him in late June, 1861, to find him just com-pleting his message to the special session opening on July 4. "The result of this war is a question of resources," said the President. "That side will win in the end where the money holds out longest; but if the war should continue until it costs us *five hundred millions of dollars*" (dwelling on this sum with emphasis, as if it were the largest amount conceivable) "the resources of the country are such that the credit of the Government will be better than it was at the close of the Revolution." Yet in the end a sum much nearer five thousand millions was required. Like others North and South, Lincoln thought the war would be short when it should have been plain it would be long. Too little and too late must be our verdict on various measures of 1861 and 1862.

In dealing with military affairs his general conception was quite sound. Thus he wrote Don Carlos Buell early in the war a correct statement of the problem. "I state my own idea of this war to be," he declared, "that we have the greater num-bers, and the enemy have the greater facility of concentrating forces upon points of collision; that we must fail unless we have some way of making our advantage an overmatch for his; and that this can only be done by menacing him with superior forces at different points at the same time . . ." In other

words, the North must make the most of its superior num-
bers, and must minimize the Southern advantage of inside
lines.

Lincoln is not to be blamed because in a few instances public opinion took a military decision out of his hands. After
Bull Run, General Winfield Scott burst out: "I am the greatest coward in America. I have fought this battle, sir, against
my judgment; I think the President of the United States ought
to remove me today for doing it." In this statement lay an
implied rebuke to Lincoln and his associates. Scott had advised
against an offensive thrust into Virginia in July, 1861, on
military grounds; Lincoln and his Cabinet had overruled Scott
on political grounds, declaring that the public would brook no
further delay. The event had proved Scott right, but the real
culprit was the public which had responded so excitably to the
cry of "On to Richmond!" Nor could Lincoln be blamed
because one commander after another, McClellan, Pope, Burn-
side, Meade, fell short of what was expected of him.

But he could be censured for some very unhappy inter-
ferences with military strategy. What, for example, of his
division of the command in western Virginia in 1862 among
Frémont, Banks, and McDowell? More distinctly, perhaps, he
can be censured, as General Sir Frederick Maurice shows, for
not finding a means of conveying his entirely sound ideas of
general policy, and his clear grasp of political necessities, to
his earlier generals. The failure of Lincoln and McClellan to
understand each other may have been mainly the fault of
McClellan, but it was partly the fault of Lincoln; and when
in 1864 a complete understanding was reached with the commander, Lincoln knowing how to give advice and support to

Grant, and Grant knowing how to give information to Lincoln, the highroad to victory was open.

2

Yet in the field of practical statesmanship these shortcomings, and still others which we could easily define, were far more than counterbalanced by Lincoln's supreme dexterity in managing both his associates and the mass opinion of the country. At first hesitant, he quickly became a true leader, relying more and more on his own judgment as he found that it was better than Seward's, Blair's, McClellan's, or Halleck's. Before long, in Gideon Welles's phrase, he had developed "wonderful self-reliance." He became the indispensable man of the crisis. "He could have dispensed with any one of his cabinet," writes Welles, "and the administration [would] not have been impaired, but it would have been difficult if not impossible to have selected anyone who could have filled the office of chief magistrate as successfully as Mr. Lincoln." Above all, he was never too far ahead of the plain people and never once behind them. A revealing document is the voluminous diary kept during the war by George Templeton Strong, a Wall Street lawyer of aristocratic connections and intellectual tastes. He saw much of Lincoln, and as treasurer of the Sanitary Commission repeatedly talked with him. At the outset, he was distrustful of the man; Lincoln seemed untutored, inexperienced, and inadequate. As the conflict continued, however, Strong's admiration increased. At the end, under date of May 14, 1865, we find him writing of a friend, General Martin T. McMahon, who had accompanied Lincoln's funeral train westward:

He says nothing in all this unprecedented manifestation of public mourning has impressed him so much as the sight that was frequent along the line of the railroad of some solitary husband-man laying down his spade or hoe or stopping his team half a mile away, taking off his hat, and remaining uncovered while the train passed by and as long as it was in sight. No prince, no leader of a people, was ever so lamented as this unpolished Western lawyer was and is. His name is Faithful and True. He will stand in history beside Washington, perhaps higher.

The terrible difficulty of this task of controlling public opinion, which meant swaying Congress and the elections of 1862 and 1864, is not easily grasped. We must remember the complete failure of Madison to preserve a decent national unity in the War of 1812, and the partial failure of Polk in the Mexican War, both acting under conditions far simpler. The war was a political war, that is, dominated by political factors. In a conflict with a foreign power national unity is seldom so difficult to attain as in an intestinal war, where large factions almost always sympathize with those in revolt. Yet without a fair degree of political unity in 1861–1865, the government would break down; without popular zeal to furnish volunteers and popular resolution to endure a draft, the armies would melt away; without general willingness to pay cruel taxes, the national effort would sink in ruin. The war, so far as possible, had to be a war of the whole people. It could not be a Republican war, but must embrace all loyal Democrats. Still less could it be a war by and for Radical Republicans, as Chase, Sumner, and Wade desired, or by and for conservative Republicans, as Seward sometimes seemed to wish. The moment Lincoln seemed to give the war effort a partisan or factional direction, he and the country were lost.

It was therefore proper that a preponderance of Lincoln's thinking and toils should be bent toward the attainment and preservation of harmony. When Oliver P. Morton, a former Democrat who became the able war governor of Indiana, complained of arms shortages, Lincoln returned a patient explanation that the country did not have munitions enough for all; that it must share them around; that the points of greatest danger needed them most; and that Indiana was far safer than Washington, where he sat within sound of the cannon of a hostile army of one hundred thousand men. "I am compelled to watch all points," he said. All points indeed! He became the grand harmonizer of the North. He had to deal with Congress, where factions snarled at each other and the Radicals set up their Committee on the Conduct of the War to snap at his heels. He had to deal with impatient New Englanders, reluctant border-State men, selfish business interests, venomous New York and Ohio Copperheads, and a dozen other elements. Once, in the summer of 1864, beset by the McClellan Democrats on one side and the Frémont Radicals on the other, he almost despaired, but even that crisis he surmounted.

Any reader of Lincoln's wartime letters must be struck by one fact: the extent to which they are addressed, not to his friends, but to his opponents and critics. All readers must be struck by another characteristic: the refusal in these letters to assert that he had been right, or his critics wrong, or in any way to address himself to posterity. After the election of 1864 he explicitly said that he would not take the victory as personal; that it "is no pleasure to me to triumph over anyone"; and that "so long as I have been here, I have not willingly planted a thorn in any man's bosom." After Appomattox he told an audience that all credit went to the army; "no part of the honor, for plan or execution, is mine." Readers of the letters must also note that, while not neglecting appeals to the sympathy, the pride, and even the fears of recipients, they emphasized cool persuasion and objective argument. As Nicolay and Hay write: "To still the quarrels of factions, to allay the jealousies of statesmen, to compose the rivalries of generals, to soothe the vanity of officials, to prompt the laggard, to curb the ardent, to sustain the faltering, was a substratum of daily routine underlying the great events of campaigns, battles, and high questions of state."

Was it easy? When we see that he never really failed to keep both the masses and the best intelligence of the country with him, we may think it was. But any tendency to believe this is quickly checked by a glance at the course and fortunes of his associates, not one of whom showed a tithe of his skill in solidifying public opinion, and several of whom proved that they were almost wholly out of touch with it.

How completely Seward's famous letter of April 1, 1861, for example, suggesting the propriety of provoking a European war in the hope of thus reuniting the North and South against a common enemy, would have destroyed all public confidence in the Secretary had it been known! Seward owed it to Lincoln's magnanimity and his desire for national unity that the country did not hear of that letter until a generation later, when Nicolay and Hay astounded their readers by publishing it. The elder Charles Francis Adams delivered a Memorial Address on William H. Seward in 1873 in which he made an unhappy attempt to arrogate the chief credit for the merits of the Lincoln Administration to the New Yorker. It fell to the second Charles Francis Adams, in his life of his father, to describe how Seward in his famous Dispatch No. 10, dated May 21, 1861, repeated the blunder of April 1, and how this bellicose paper, which Lincoln first drastically toned down, and then earmarked to be held confidential and secret in the London legation, was entirely misconceived by the minister to England. Adams thought it had been dictated by an impetuous Lincoln!

. . . It puzzled and dismayed Mr. Adams when he first received it. The fiercely aggressive, the well-nigh inconceivable, foreign policy it foreshadowed must, he thought, have been forced on the Secretary by the other members of the administration; but, in fact, though Mr. Adams never knew it, that dispatch, in the form in which it was originally drawn up by the Secretary of State and by him submitted to the President, must have been designed to precipitate a foreign war. Moreover, it would inevitably have brought about that result but for Lincoln's unseen intervention.

Seward's impetuosity, if known, would twice have ruined him in the eyes of all sober Northerners. Nor was the accomplished Secretary Chase happier in dealing with Congressional and public opinion. His conduct of the Treasury was in general admirable. He was a man of perfect integrity, great ability, and marked persistence. But he had no powers of persuasion whatever; his relations with Congress show an unbroken record of mutual distrust and bitter wrangling; although he matured a comprehensive scheme for financing the war as early as December, 1861, he could get no Congressional group to support it; and he was totally unable to raise up devoted lieutenants either in politics or in his Treasury work. He knew so little of public sentiment that he entertained the preposterous idea in 1864 that he might supplant Lincoln; and when he resigned that summer he was astonished to find most of the press and other indexes of opinion blithely content to let him go. Montgomery Blair, to take another instance, belonged to a family of highly astute politicians. Yet he committed acts, such as delivering a needless speech on miscegenation, which angered great segments of the public; he was quite unable to get along with other men, denouncing Chase, Seward, and others in violent terms; and after he had assailed Stanton as a "coward and poltroon," his exit from the Cabinet caused much rejoicing and little mourning.

We may compare with the woeful indiscretions of these men, and the story of their failure to gain any wide hold on public affection, the skill with which Lincoln dealt with the most distinctive feature of his Administration, the proclamation of emancipation. The most dangerous subject that any leader could touch, emancipation seemed a three-edged sword, likely to give a mortal wound to any user. First, in the critical border States it affected the property of tens of thousands of the most influential men, and the social interests of nearly all white people. Second, to resort to emancipation meant changing the objects of the war, which had been begun as a struggle to maintain the Union and was now turned into an onslaught against slavery. And third, most Democrats and many conservative Republicans would protest that emancipation was a betrayal of the solemn pledge in the Crittenden resolution which had been voted by an almost unanimous Congress in 1861—a declaration that the war would be fought *only* for the Union.

Yet under the inexorable pressure of events the subject had to be grappled with. Late spring of 1862 found Lincoln, aware that the hour of decision was near, striving to appraise a broad complex of forces and to gauge a crescent change in public feeling. The war had initiated a revolution in Northern thinking upon slavery, and as General Hunter's attempt to free many of the slaves in South Carolina followed that of Frémont to liberate some of them in Missouri, the popular response showed that the torrent of this revolution was carrying great sections of the population with it. As the fighting went on, the masses were saying to themselves: "Slavery is the cause of this horrible contest; it is slavery that is maiming the republic, impoverishing the taxpayer, and filling the land with widows and orphans. We must strike at the roots of our calamity—we must extinguish slavery."

Lincoln, watching the current, had to seize the precise moment for effective action. Mignet, in his history of the French Revolution, remarks: "A man is sometimes a mere feather in an upheaval which carries away the masses; the surge sweeps him along, or leaves him overwhelmed behind; he must keep in advance or be trampled under foot." Despite all Lincoln's reluctance to touch an institution protected by the Constitution, despite his doubts both as to expediency and legal power, he had to keep in mind the truth which Mignet enunciated. It was true that if he moved too soon, conservative men would raise the cry of rash and arbitrary usurpation, and voters would perhaps respond in savage force on election day in 1862. But if he waited too long, majority opinion would follow the Radicals in losing patience with him, and he would be left "overwhelmed behind." He had to understand what the average sentiment of the country would approve, and to mold and guide that sentiment. Simultaneously he had to watch the course of the war, for while he could proclaim emancipation in the moment of victory, he could not do it in the moment of military defeat. He was coming to the rescue of Ethiopia; he must not let it seem that he was calling on Ethiopia to rise and rescue him.

Always a believer in gradualism, Lincoln to the very end of the war thought that gradual emancipation, with compensation to all loyal owners and perhaps all owners loyal or disloyal, would be fairer to the Southern white man, to the Negro, and to the nation as a whole than a sudden destruction of slavery. Be it remembered that he genuinely believed that the Southern masses had been misled by agitators and demagogues. Be it remembered that he was always specially respectful of the border region, where he had been born, and which was represented in his Cabinet by two members, Edward Bates and Montgomery Blair.

He had made repeated appeals to the border States to accept the plan for gradual emancipation, with the aid and cooperation of the general government, which he had persuaded Congress to endorse. On May 19, 1862, he publicly and earnestly besought the border Congressmen to yield to this plan on the ground, among others, that it would shorten the war; for the Southern leaders, if they once saw that Kentucky, Missouri, and Maryland were irretrievably lost, would more readily give up their revolt. And still again, on July 12, calling the border Representatives to the White House, he pleaded with them for acceptance of the scheme. "I assure you," he said, "that, in my opinion, if you had all voted for the resolution in the gradual emancipation message of last March, the war would now be substantially ended." But the border men still resisted his entreaties.

For a variety of reasons the reluctant President could not

wait longer; he had to keep at the head of opinion. One reason lay in the fact that the war itself was destroying slavery. Wherever the Union armies penetrated, they abolished servitude, as Lincoln put it, by mere "friction and abrasion." When Port Royal was captured in South Carolina, thousands of Negroes poured into the military camps; and it was partly for this reason that General Hunter issued his much-applauded order of May, 1862, freeing the slaves of South Carolina, Georgia, and Florida wherever they were reached by Northern forces. Lincoln had to revoke that order, but he could not revoke the conditions that elicited it.

As another reason, it was now evident that the war would be long, bloody, and expensive. When McClellan lost his Peninsular campaign, all hope of an early termination of the contest perished. If it were to be long and bloody, emancipation would be justified as a war measure; for it would add to the resources of the North in man power, it would, perhaps, create restlessness among the slaves in certain Southern areas, and, above all, transcending every other consideration, it would put moral purpose into the war. It would give millions of Americans a sense that they were fighting a war of human liberation; it would be hailed in Europe as a Messianic edict, closing an unhappy era in the life of the world's most hopeful nation, and opening a shining new chapter—redeeming the promise of American democracy to the world. Finally, it would meet the more and more exigent demand of Northern opinion, now so steadily crystallizing.

Thus it was that on September 22, 1862, Lincoln devoted the whole strength of the North to the fulfillment of a promise that: "On the first day of January in the year of our Lord one thousand eight hundred and sixty-three, all persons held as slaves within any State or designated part of a State, the people whereof shall then be in rebellion against the United States, shall be then, thenceforward, and forever free." All students of history have agreed that the step was taken at precisely the right moment, and in precisely the right way. It was not taken too soon, or until all decent alternatives had been thoroughly explored. It was assuredly not taken a moment too late.

Much has been written about the limitations of the great proclamation. It did not free the slaves in those areas which had never "rebelled," nor in districts where the "rebellion" had been suppressed. In sober fact, it applied to the slaves only in areas where the national government as yet had no authority. Yet it was nevertheless an immortal blow for human freedom. It not only changed the aims of the war, but it raised them to a higher level. Infusing a new moral meaning into the conflict, it deepened that element of passion and inspiration which vibrated in so many of Lincoln's utterances. It rallied the liberal thought of Britain and the globe to the Union side. Month by month, year by year, it had a widening influence. "Great," wrote Emerson, "is the virtue of this Proclamation. It works when men are sleeping, when the army goes into winter quarters, when generals are treacherous or imbecile." In its way, it is working still.

Yet the idea that the Southern people had rights in the matter which should be respected was one which Lincoln never lost. When he talked with Alexander H. Stephens at the Hampton Roads conference in 1865, he took care to explain his course and expound his future hopes. Thus, writes Stephens:

He said it was not his intention in the beginning to interfere with slavery in the States; that he never would have done it, if he had not been compelled by necessity to do it, to maintain the Union; that the subject presented many difficult and perplexing questions to him, that he had hesitated for some time, and had resorted to this measure, only when driven to it by public necessity; that he had been in favor of the General Government prohibiting the extension of slavery into the Territories, but did not think that that Government possessed power over the subject in the States, except as a war measure; and that he had always himself been in favor of emancipation, but not immediate emancipation, even by the States.

He went on to say that he would be willing to be taxed to remunerate the Southern people for their slaves. He believed that the people of the North were as responsible for slavery as the people of the South, and if the war should then cease, with the voluntary abolition of slavery by the States, he should be in favor, individually, of the Government paying a fair indemnity for the loss to the owners. He said he believed this feeling had an extensive existence at the North. He knew some who would be in favor of an appropriation as high as four hundred millions of dollars for this purpose.

This passage, so clearly stamped by kindliness toward the Southern people, brings us to another consideration. As it was Jefferson Davis's special task to create a nation, it was Lincoln's to maintain a nation; to consolidate Northern sentiment, to lift the Northern heart, and to keep an effective Northern majority behind him. He did it by sagacious measures, and by a constant appeal to idealism and moral passion of the people. But it was not merely the internal harmony of the

North of which he thought; he equally kept in mind the
future harmony of the whole nation. He looked forward to
a restoration not merely of the physical Union, but of the
old Union of hearts and affections. The nation could not long
be pinned together by bayonets; it would have to be pinned
together by the common memories, common culture and
ideas, and common aims in building the future, which had
been the cement of Union in the past. Throughout the conflict he never indulged in any word that would heighten the
tides of anger, vengefulness, and malice that swept the land.
On the contrary, he always tried to repress sectional animosi-
ties, reduce the hatreds of war, and mollify the nation's temper. Jefferson Davis several times heaped bitter imprecations
upon the North; but Lincoln never once spoke unkindly of
the Southern people, and never went beyond a measured
severity even in condemning those he considered their worst
demagogues. As James G. Randall puts it:

In earliest life, in years of growth, in love and friendship, in
the family circle, in the tough substance of democratic thought,
Lincoln's mind and character were moulded by Southern influences. In wistfulness for other days when sectionalism was rag-
ing, in the midst of tragic strife as at Gettysburg, where he uttered
not a syllable of hatred, Lincoln gave evidence of Southern understanding. In his closeness to border State opinion, in his design
for freedom, in incidents of presidential helpfulness to friends on
the other side, and at the last in his pattern for peace without
vindictiveness, Lincoln kept his sympathy for the people of the
South.

This course was an essential part of his statesmanship. He
had to preserve a nation; and the only nation worth preserving

was one of brotherly kinship and affection. Campbell-Bannerman during the South African War was profoundly aware that the Boers would have to be lived with after the conflict; he indulged in no unkind word or gesture; the Afrikanders, he said, "must be taken to our bosom." He was but following Lincoln's example.

The golden thread of concern for national unity can be traced through the whole administration. In December, 1861, Lincoln told Congress that three vacancies existed in the Supreme Court. "I have so far forborne from making nominations to fill these vacancies," he added, "for reasons which I will now state. Two of the outgoing judges resided within the States now overrun by revolt; so that if successors were appointed in the same localities, they could not now serve upon their circuits; and many of the most competent men there probably would not take the personal hazard of accepting to serve, even here, upon the Supreme Bench. I have been unwilling to throw all the appointments northward, thus disabling myself from doing justice to the South on the return of peace; although I may remark that to transfer to the North one which has heretofore been in the South would not, with reference to territory and population, be unjust."

We can guess how happy Lincoln would have been could he have known that before many decades elapsed a Louisianian would be Chief Justice. In 1863, just after Gettysburg, General Meade issued some general orders which both pained and irritated Lincoln; for in these orders Meade spoke of "driving the invaders from our soil." To Lincoln every foot of the nation's land was "our soil"—and this unhappy phrase rankled in his mind as he wrote a stern letter of rebuke to Meade. We all know how mild and generous was Lincoln's plan of reconstruction, and how mildly and generously he had it applied, first in Louisiana, then in Arkansas, and lastly in Tennessee. We all know how decisively he intervened on behalf of the South when Congress in the Wade-Davis bill of 1864 arrogated to itself (quite unconstitutionally, as Lincoln believed) the power to destroy slavery within the States, and prescribed a much harsher scheme of reconstruction. His secretaries preserve the constitutional lesson he administered to Zack Chandler:

Chandler: "The important point [in the bill] is that one prohibiting slavery in the reconstructed States."

Lincoln: "This is the very point on which I doubt the authority of Congress to act."

Chandler: "It is no more than you have done yourself!"

Lincoln: "I conceive that I may in an emergency do things on military grounds which cannot be done constitutionally by Congress."

Few scenes in our Presidential history are so remarkable as that of the first Cabinet meeting after the Hampton Roads Conference, at which Lincoln had talked of peace with Alexander H. Stephens and R. M. T. Hunter. The date was February 5, 1865; Southern defeat was now certain; it was clear that the spring offensive would bring the fall of Richmond. Lee's surrender was in fact but two months away. Yet to that night meeting of the Cabinet Lincoln submitted a plan for paying $400,000,000 to the Southern States, in proportion to their slave populations, in return for an early termination of hostilities; all political offenses to be pardoned, and all property except slaves to be released from confiscation or forfeiture. It is clear that he had a larger object in view than the shortening of the war by a few weeks. He wished to bring the Southern States back on terms that fell short of total subjugation; to give the impoverished Southern people a fund with which to begin rebuilding their economy; and by an act of sweeping generosity to lay the foundation for a Union of hearts, not of force. His regret when the Cabinet unanimously disapproved of his plan was strongly expressed, and for a time he hoped to revive it. One of his last acts on the day of his assassination was to hold a conference with James W. Singleton, once of Virginia and later of Quincy, Illinois, on plans for reconstructing Virginia under the Pierpont Government.

It was with good reason that the Richmond *Whig* began its editorial of Monday, April 17, on the assassination of Lincoln, with the words: "The heaviest blow which has ever fallen upon the people of the South has descended."

All this is proof of Lincoln's statesmanship—but he was something more than a statesman. Herbert Croly included in his book, *The Promise of American Life*, a chapter entitled "Lincoln As More Than an American"—one of the best short estimates of Lincoln's career ever written. His thesis was that while Lincoln is often called a typical American, in actuality he was very untypical. In an era and region where most men looked down upon education—at any rate, any high degree of education—he carefully trained and filled his mind; using for this purpose precisely the right instruments—Euclid, who taught him exactness; the Bible, which taught him moral elevation; and Shakespeare, who taught him humanity. In an environment where men were careless and undisciplined, Lincoln trained himself to be highly self-controlled, patient, and watchful. At a time when the country admired reckless, aggressive, self-willed men like Jackson, Lincoln was mag-

nanimous, thoughtful, considerate of every interest, and re-
strained. Croly's appraisal was just—Lincoln was a good deal
more than a typical American. For somewhat different reasons,
we may say that he was more than a statesman—more than a
Bismarck or Cavour.

4

A supreme realist, in one respect he was often ready to
abandon realism. That is, he was ready, on fit occasion, to
appeal to a spirit of idealism and generosity which hardly
existed—which was almost imperceptible—but which his appeal could sometimes call into being; a coal of finer feeling
which his example and his simple eloquence could sometimes
fan into flame. We have said that he almost always addressed
himself to men who differed from him, not to friends, and that
he appealed to their reason, not their prejudices and emotions. He did more than this: he appealed to their better selves.
And his appeal to the country at large was an appeal to its
nobler side, its better nature.

In three positive respects he tried to awaken the idealism
and enlarge the vision of the people. To begin with, he never
ceased to tell the Northerners, at least after the summer of
1862, that the struggle they were maintaining was essentially
a moral struggle. He thought it a plain moral axiom that the
black man should have the same right as the white man to eat
the bread he had earned by the sweat of his brow. He wanted
all men everywhere to be free. He knew that the North was
as responsible for slavery as the South; he tolerated it as a
parent would tolerate a snake found in bed with the children—
it must be killed in a way that would not inflict needless

injury on those burdened with it; but he always thought the institution, as an institution, immoral.

In the second instance, Lincoln never ceased to insist that the war was a struggle for the vindication of democracy in the sight of all mankind; a war for the renovation of democratic government, so that its example could be kept effective to all other peoples. When at Gettysburg he interpreted the meaning of the conflict, it was in these terms of the necessity of preserving the great American example for the struggling and oppressed of other lands. The dead had given the last full measure of devotion not merely for the Union, and not merely for the ending of slavery, but that the nation should have a rebirth of freedom, and that popular government should lift a brighter torch than ever. The survival of that government with undimmed lustre actually was of the first importance to struggling democracy in Great Britain, in France, and in other lands. If, in the Grant Administration, the torch burned with a murky stench, it was still there, and men knew that the flame could be purified, as in no great time it was.

And, in the third instance, Lincoln more than once touched upon a yet larger concept. He had a vision of the immense and he hoped gradually brightening future of mankind. Indeed, he alone among nineteenth century statesmen after the generation of Madison and Jefferson seems to have had that vision. He realized that the political and social life of mankind is only in its beginnings, that it will develop through long ages to come, and that we do not act for our generation or the next alone but for countless generations to follow. In his letter of May 19, 1862, he had appealed to the border States to adopt gradual emancipation in just these terms. They must do their duty with a sense that it would affect coming centuries, ran his argument. "May the vast future not have to lament that you have neglected it."

He saw that the American conflict, so terrible an agony to those caught in its coils, would yet appear but as one brief event in the long march of mankind to happier goals. His fullest expression of his concept appeared in his noble letter of August 26, 1863, to J. C. Conkling of Springfield; a letter written when the nation had emerged from the terrible anxieties of Gettysburg and Vicksburg to find that its path ahead seemed clearer. "The signs look better," wrote Lincoln, in phrasing worthy of Shakespeare:

The Father of Waters again goes unvexed to the sea. Thanks to the great Northwest for it; nor yet wholly to them. Three hundred miles up they met New England, Empire, Keystone, and Jersey, hewing their way right and left. The sunny South, too, in more colors than one, lent a helping hand. On the spot their part of the history was jotted down in black and white. The job was a great national one, and let none be slighted who bore an honorable part in it. And while those who have cleared the great river may well be proud, even that is not all. It is hard to say that anything has been more bravely or well done than at Antietam, Murfreesboro, Gettysburg, and on many fields of less note. Nor must Uncle Sam's web feet be forgotten. At all the watery margins they have been present, not only on the deep sea, the broad bay, and the rapid river, but also up the narrow muddy bayou, and wherever the ground was a little damp, they have been and made their tracks.

And then came the climactic sentence, one of the noblest Lincoln ever wrote:

Thanks to all. For the great Republic,—for the principle it lives by and keeps alive,—for man's vast future,—thanks to all.

In this concept that the American Civil War was a struggle for the future of humanity, Lincoln joined hands with the Revolutionary statesmen—Washington, Jefferson, Madison, Adams—who had a vision of the creation of a new and brighter civilization; who believed that they were throwing open the gates to a higher, better future for all men. He became more than a statesman—he was a seer, a prophet, a poet. Recently, since 1950, American boys have died in the rice fields and on the mountains of Korea—for what? For the United States, for justice and democracy, but above all for a still larger cause—for the United Nations and for the orderly free progress of mankind.

We Americans shall doubtless meet great crises in the future, as we have met them in the past. In some of these crises, no doubt, superhuman exertions may well again be needed. To those who will have to bear the strain and agony, there will echo down the inspiring words of the great seer of the year 1863: "Thanks to all. For the great Republic,—for the principle it lives by and keeps alive,—*for man's vast future*,—thanks to all."

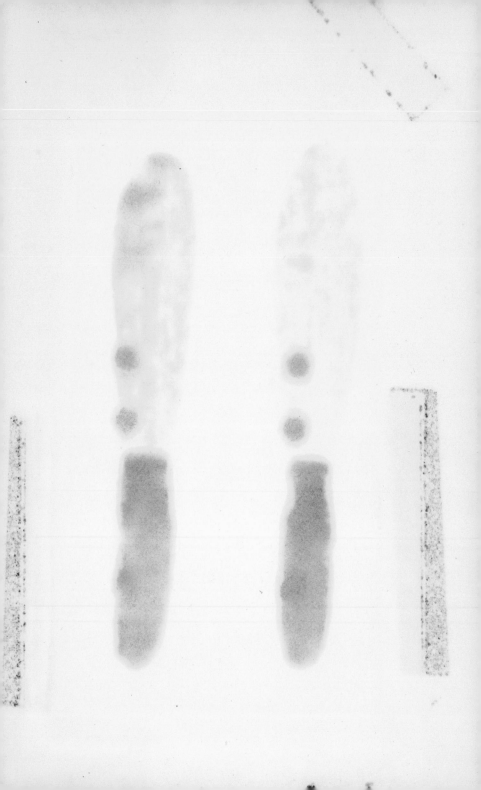

1/24/54

34136

E
458
N45

NEVINS, ALLAN
    THE STATESMANSHIP OF
THE CIVIL WAR.

DATE DUE

Fernald Library
Colby-Sawyer College
New London, New Hampshire

GAYLORD   PRINTED IN U.S.A.